T0128433

SEEKING HIGHER GROUND

DON POOLE

WESTBOW PRESS®
A DIVISION OF THOMAS NELSON & ZONDERVAN

WestBow Press books may be ordered through booksellers or by contacting:

WestBow Press
A Division of Thomas Nelson & Zondervan
1663 Liberty Drive
Bloomington, IN 47403
www.westbowpress.com
1 (866) 928-1240

ISBN: 978-1-9736-5715-6 (sc)
ISBN: 978-1-9736-5714-9 (e)

Print information available on the last page.

WestBow Press rev. date: 3/19/2019

CONTENTS

PREFACE

As Wesley says in "The Princess Bride;[1]" "No one of consequence." I am a retired teacher, in his seventies, and I taught science for 28 years straight. I was a trainer of teachers and administrators for 13 years after that. I went to many foreign countries to train teachers and administrators in the 'break-away' Soviet Union. I have traveled to such faraway places as Mongolia and Kazakhstan. I have taught thinking skills in the International Baccalaureate Program. I have been an observer of human behavior for more than seventy years. I have a masters degree in science education and an EBD (Everything But Dissertation) for a doctorate degree. However, one of my sons has one. (Does that count at all?) So, I guess, I really am someone of 'no consequence.' I am not an expert in any field. I am sure I don't want to be one. Too much pressure.

When I was a public-school teacher, I was what they used to call a 'constructivist.' In other words, I was very interested in what was going on in a student(s) mind when they did not understand an idea or concept that I was teaching. I would ask them questions in order for me to more fully understand their thinking process. You see, I believe that everyone 'constructs' their knowledge in a different way. That each one of us is unique in that construction of knowledge. Hence, a 'constructivist.' This uniqueness is what I believe gives us our creativity that we can share with the world. What I learned from my life experiences is that people tend to 'fall' into thinking patterns that are destructive of their behavior and

[1] "The Princess Bride;" Twentieth Century Fox; 1987.

their world view. Some of these patterns are more dangerous than others. Concepts that I have learned to question in our culture you may find highly questionable about me. Some of these are: cuteness, simplicity, sentimentality, patriotism, just to name a few. Some of you are probably thinking: "What could be wrong with 'cuteness' or patriotism or simplicity?" Just you wait.

You may be thinking that the title for this book is rather a lot to handle; Higher Ground and the like. But don't get me wrong, I am not providing any higher truth in this book, that part is up to you. I am just attempting to level your playing/thinking field so you can seek the higher truth. Hopefully I can provide some insight into your thinking patterns to become tools for your thinking. My attempt here is to help you think in what I think are more constructive ways about the world around you.

I have watched friends in my life go down thinking paths that have cut them off from 'reality' ("What a concept!" Thanks Robin Williams). This thinking put my friends in 'Scrooge' like places in their lives (Thanks Charles Dickens). I hope you notice that I am using metaphors in this introduction that take you down a thought pattern just by their mention. Our minds are very quick to learn. We search for patterns in the world around us, so we can make 'sense' of it all. The problem is that we often jump to conclusions about these patterns we have discovered. So then, some of us end up down a path of thinking that leads to our own personal version of reality. And more problematic, we don't question how we got there.

By now, you have noticed that I use the punctuation '' often around a word. When I do that, my purpose is to let the reader know that the word with this punctuation around it has several meanings depending on the context used, and/or the word has an emotional 'charge' on it. By emotional 'charge,' I mean that the word has either negative or positive connotations to it, depending on your experiences. So then, how I am using a word with apostrophes around it means there are other contexts that the word has, but please use the one that I am inferring.

My writing style is a cross between 'stream of consciousness' and informal word usage. My English teachers tried to train me, but I resisted. However, I did enjoy their abilities at word-smithing (akin to blacksmithing[2]; hammering out a well-structured sentence!). I try to learn a new word each day, or review a word that I don't use in my everyday vocabulary. One of my concerns in our present culture is the 'dumbing down' of our common vocabulary through such technological 'advances' as texting and social media, which have accelerated our use of a less extensive vocabulary. As George Orwell pointed out so clearly in his book: Nineteen Eighty-four (his book not the year!), when a culture has a small vocabulary, that culture is easily manipulated. This is true, I believe, because this small vocabulary forces the mind to think in a limited number of pathways. And the more pathways we have in our thinking, the more analytical and accurate we can be in our interpretation of reality. In another sense I am asking you to 'repent.' Now when you hear that term you probably think of a church service or a 'revival' meeting where you are asked to come forward and commit your life to God. That isn't what I am talking about. I am using the word 'repent' in the original meaning: to think about the way you think. If you notice the word 'repent' has the suffix 'pent' in it that comes from the word pensive, meaning to think about something. Look it up. That's another thing I do; ask you to 'look it up.' Don't just take my word for something, explore the meaning(s) on your own.

My main objective in this book is to help 'rein in' the runaway thinking patterns that are causing much division in our culture, our America.

Some of you may note that my bibliography mostly contains books written some time ago. You might conclude that I am an old person caught in my past, and that may be true, but I am also a

[2] I put a footnote here because I am not sure if a lot of people know what a blacksmith is... look it up!

person who realizes that many good source books were written in the past, and remain relevant for today. My annotated bibliography contains what for me are 'oldies but goodies,' and I quote them in this book.

I have known that something was wrong in the American Christian churches for a long time. I just didn't know what. When I spoke to 'church' members that were dividing themselves on the basis of 'conservative' and 'liberal,' I suspected something was wrong. When I talked with old friends who had no problem with America 'getting even' with terrorists around the world by resorting to the violence that had created them in the first place, I knew something was wrong. When I talked with 'Christian' friends of mine who were willing to vote for people who were immoral, crude and inflammatory, I knew something was wrong in Christianity. When my son (the pastor) and I both came to the conclusion that we did not want to be identified by the term 'Christian' anymore, because of its political football status, I knew something was wrong. Then I read the book *Resident Aliens*[3]. What is described in that book gave me a clear understanding of the problem. The 'Church' had become complicit in American politics and not the politics of Jesus. Both the 'conservative' and 'liberal' churches have been serving the needs of American politicians and they have become their 'servants,' and not the servants of the American people.[4]

There is a town in Maryland which has an American flag and a Cross alongside each other, on a hill overlooking the town. The cross and the flag are almost the same size. For me, this represented the problem in the American Christian churches. These churches have assumed that we could serve both God and country equally. They were both gods. One god occasionally demanded the sacrifice of our sons and daughters, the other only if they left the security

[3] S. Hauerwas & W.H. Willimon, *Resident Aliens* (Abingdon Press, 2014)

[4] See Matthew 23:11. NIV

of our country and became missionaries. As 'Christians' we had forgotten who Jesus was. He was our personal savior and not the Lord of our lives. The churches in America were relegated to a private religion, where it could not offer an alternative to the 'world.' Christianity dealt with 'spiritual' things, while America dealt with 'reality.' What American Christians fail to understand is that the universe is based upon 'spiritual' things.[5]

When I took a vow as a Christian (when I joined a church) I professed that Jesus is my Lord and savior. But, was Jesus really my LORD? I think not. The ten commandments begin with the commandment: "You will have no other gods before Me.[6]" Since Jesus is God, as a 'Christian' I should have no other gods before Him. Putting my country equal with God amounts to the same thing as idol worship. The problem is that I had been doing this for so long, that I didn't even realize I was doing it. It had been ingrained in me since I first attended Sunday school and public school, as I pledged allegiance to the flag and a Bible verse was read before classes began.[7] God and country had become equal gods in my mind. An assumption that I did not examine for over 70 years!

So, I no longer wish to be called a 'Christian,' but prefer to be called a follower of Jesus, or FOJ for short. As long as 'Christianity' is just a religion, it can blend into American society and its pastors and leaders can have TV shows, rather than going to jail, as they originally did in the early church. We have been 'tamed' and not a threat to the governments of the world, because we 'support' our politicians and nation. In fact, we have become nothing more than a tool in the hands of our politicians. The 'conservative' churches have hijacked God for their own purposes, and the 'liberal' churches have relegated God to a 'personal' choice (just don't talk about it).

---

[5] See section of this book on "What is Information."

[6] Ex 20:3 NIV

[7] I know that is no longer true for every school, but it was when I was a kid.

So, this pretty much defines for me what the problem is in American Christian churches. We must reclaim our position of being an alternative way to live, following the commands of Jesus and not the commands of our nation. We are to be 'resident aliens,' pointing to another way to live with Jesus as our LORD and savior.

I am not clear on how to refer to God in this book. So, I may use terms that may cause you to pause and question my thinking on how to refer to God. Since I believe that God is the Ultimate Being, I think God is better described by what God is not, then by what God is. I may use a term for God like 'I AM.[8]' I may use 'I AM' to refer to God, since God is present throughout His universe. I don't use the term 'I AM' as way to make God less, but quite the opposite. Sometimes I use the term 'He/She' just to make a point. Please don't take my usage as sacrilegious, that is not my intent.

Also, I use a lot of footnotes. **It would be very helpful, that as you read my text, you attend to my footnotes as you go. They add further insight into my thinking.**

I still remember vividly the night I presented our science curriculum for the parents at back to school night when I was 24 years old. I had taught seventh grade science that year. When I had finished my presentation, a parent raised his hand and wanted to know why I had taught about the 'origin of life' and didn't mention God? This question was followed by a chorus of murmurings of agreement around this parent. I don't remember what I said, only the confusion and awkwardness of the moment. The next morning, I found pamphlets in my mailbox at school about the 'false' teachings of 'evolution' and suggesting that those who taught it were "agents of the devil." I had been attacked by the 'protectors of God's word,' as I came to learn later. I was not a 'Christian' at the time, but I was beginning to be a seeker of God. Now I see the event as a positive note in my personal search for

[8] I choose a capitalized gender-neutral term for God, since this is how God told Moses a name: "I AM." See Ex 3:13-14 NIV

"truth" in whatever form it would take. But then, that event did more damage than good. I was a victim and soldier in the 'Bible War' (only I didn't know it).

For the next 50 or more years, I have read book after book on theology and science, sometimes separately and more recently together. Of course, I found myself reading more of the authors in tune with my personal mental framework, and less of those who did not seem to fit me, so I was slanting my viewpoint from the beginning, choosing not to read the more 'fundamentalist' views of Scripture and science. I asked in the process of reading these many books for God to guide my readings that would reinforce His WORD and speak to me through the book I was reading. Obviously, this comment will put me at odds with some Christians right away. And that is part of the problem.

I have led adult Sunday school groups and evening groups in studying the Bible and other topics of interest to adults for over 45 years on a regular basis. I have noticed over and over that there are two general types of responses to questions I have posed to groups to get them thinking. The one question that stands out to me is: "Do you think you will see Hitler in heaven?" Now that's a pretty emotionally charged question, especially to Jewish people. Well, let me tell you, I got some very different responses to that question. 1) I was a heretic and let us report you to the pastor; 2) "I never thought about that. Let's discuss it." And, there was hardly anyone in between. In my memory, I can't think of any. So, either some people didn't show up to my group next week, or they came ready to prove me wrong. The telling thing here is that I was just asking a question, not stating a belief, or saying that I had any agreement with what I asked. My objective was (in asking this question) to get people to 'think' about some assumptions they have made about their faith. But boy did I get put on the 'suspect heretic' list of some people.

Finally, this book project of mine is written with my grandchildren in mind. They are among the ones who I hope will read this book. They are where my thoughts are focused. They represent my hope for the future. Yeah, I know the song and all that sentimental stuff, but that's not my point. These grandchildren of mine are my future. They contain about ¼ of my DNA. My hope is that people who read this book can have a 'leg up' from where I am now in my life (near the end). I hope they don't need as much time as I did to figure a lot of things out about this life we share in common.

INTRODUCTION

THREE THINKING PATTERNS

Over my course in life, I have thought about thinking a lot. I have taught 'thinking skills' to students and teachers. I have studied books on the brain and the workings of the 'mind'. After a long time thinking about what is happening in the world around me, I have come up with three thinking patterns (not really styles) that seem to me to be interfering with what I would call clear thinking.

These three are: All or Nothing thinking (A/NT); Emotional thinking (ET) and Anthropomorphic[9] Thinking (AT). I will use the acronyms A/NT, ET and AT for 'simplicity' and because I don't want to write them over and over.

Now, for a brief description of each:

A/NT is when we usually put things and people in categories and say such things as all, never, always, constantly, ever, at no time, not at all, and the like. We don't see any variation in what we have classified be it things, people or events. Common examples are: "You never listen to me!" "I always lose." "All women are scatterbrained." "All black people are inferior to white people." This pattern of thinking is a lot easier to find yourself in then you may think. I find myself doing it more often when I am frustrated with people or situations. I have heard celebrities use A/NT and

[9] Ascribing human form or attributes to a being or thing not human.

not even realize that they have done it. For example, when the new African American History museum opened in Washington D. C. and Oprah Winfrey was being interviewed she said: "All my heroes are in there." All of her heroes? She doesn't have any heroes other than African Americans? I think if you were to tell her about her comment as an A/NT comment, she would correct herself. My point is that this pattern of thinking creeps into our thought a lot quicker and more ubiquitously then we realize. These comments reveal our prejudices and pecking order thinking. These A/NT thinking patterns are the beginnings of bigotry and racism in our culture. To my way of 'thinking' this is the most dangerous thinking pattern in our culture.

ET (not to be confused with Extra Terrestrial) is when our thinking is decidedly emotional. When we let our emotions rule, rather than our reasoning skills. We let the emotional part of our brain (our limbic system) make our decisions for us. For example; when asked why a woman stays with her abusive husband or boyfriend, she says: "I know he really loves me." Or "I am a vegetarian because I can't abide what people do to animals to get meat." Usually our ET is a result of events in the past that triggered our emotional sentinel; the amygdala.[10]

More needs to be said about our amygdala. This part of our emotional system in our brain can cause us to react to an event before our higher thinking centers, known as the cerebral cortex[11], can get involved. The amygdala acts as our first decision maker, and unfortunately, it is our least logical self. This is why you may find yourself blurting out comments without thinking first (using your cerebral cortex). And saying: "I can't believe I said that!" I certainly have done this and most of the time not knowing the reason. The amygdala is very good at remembering my emotional

---

[10] Amygdala-almond shaped nuclei in limbic system of brain. Responsible for formation and storage of emotional memories.

[11] The largest part of our brain, where reasoning, language, attention, perception, awareness, and in general consciousness is located.

memories from the beginning of my life and will quickly respond to emotional situations. And the important thing to remember is to learn not to immediately react to a situation but take the time to THINK BEFORE YOU ACT. Count to ten. Or whatever you can do to allow time for your cerebral cortex to kick in.

AT is when we believe that we know what is going on in the brains of other organisms. For example: "I know that my dog loves me because he/she is so excited to see me." "You can tell that frogs are stupid by the look on their face." (yes, I have actually heard a student say this). Anthropomorphism is when we put human attributes on animals and other beings, when in fact we really have no idea what is going on in their brains or being.

What all three patterns of thinking have in common is that they are based on assumptions that we make when we encounter situations or people or other organisms or things. So, I guess you could say that my whole attempt here is to lower our ability to make poor assumptions in life. My hope is that through the recognition of our thinking patterns we will raise the level of awareness in our lives.

Tony Schwarz[12] said: "Consciousness is simply the capacity to see more and include more. Against a backdrop of narrowness and blindness *at the top,*[13] consciousness is rising. It's the only thing that will defeat ignorance and evil and advance the common good." This reinforces what I mean by awareness. Our consciousness is demonstrated by our awareness of the universe around us. And the old adage that 'ignorance is bliss' is reinforced. What we don't know (our ignorance) is the measure of our unawareness. And we can never know even a fraction of all that God knows. We can only be in awe at God's level of consciousness of the universe. The greatest of poverty is unawareness (ignorance).

---

[12] Tony Schwartz, https://twitter.com; March 5, 2018. (author and journalist)

[13] Schwartz Is referring to government. (USA)

The Dominance of the Left-brain (hemisphere)

The society we live in is very left-brain oriented. What does this mean? What does the left side of your brain want? What is its purpose? I think I need to start this section with some science. First: your brain is divided into the left and right hemispheres. These two hemispheres are not symmetrical; one side is larger and weighs more than the other. You guessed it, the right side is bigger and weighs more. The left side of your brain communicates with the right side of your body and the right side of your brain communicates with the left side of your body. If a person has a massive stroke on the left side of his/her brain, the right side becomes paralyzed. Whether you are right handed or left handed has little to do with side of the brain you prefer to think out of or trust. Many of your primary cognitive functions are handled by both sides of the brain, each side handles the information from your senses differently. Linear reasoning (language/grammar) is handled primarily in the left brain and holistic reasoning (nonverbals/intonation) is handled primarily in the right brain. There is even reason to believe that each hemisphere has its own personality[14], which would explain to me why I sometimes have a 'meeting of the minds' with myself when I am making an important decision. This doesn't mean that both sides of your brain are not involved in these thinking processes. It is a common misunderstanding to think you are 'left-brained' or 'right-brained' in an A/NT way. Both hemispheres are crucial in limiting the assumptions that you make as you go about your daily life. When they are working in harmony with each other, your brain is at its optimal performance level. Below is a chart which summarizes the salient features of each hemisphere for comparison.

[14] Based on split-brain research; see footnote 15.

Left/Right Brain Hemisphere Comparison[15]

Hemisphere	Left	Right
Mental tools	• Language • Decontextualizes • Logic • Sees the 'trees' • Collect/organize/sequence • Explicit reasoning • Likes repeatability • Tool use • Strategy	• Music is its language • Contextualizes • Metaphors • Sees the 'forest' • Complex pattern recognition • More connected to the unconscious • Detects anomalies • Moral judgement • Humor/sarcasm
Major attitudes toward the world	- How do I use and control the world? - Likes "I know" rather than "I believe." - (Belief is a feeble form of knowing.) - Uncertainty is to be avoided. - Optimistic - Has the end point in view - Denial (a source of addiction)	- Relationship of care for the world. - Likes "I believe" or "I think." - Uncertainty is a reality. - Desire and longing - Empathy - Sense of self
Mediation of experience	1. Depends on denotative language and abstraction. 2. Yields clarity and power to use things that are known, static and lifeless. 3. Engaged in purpose and usefulness. 4. Most active in confabulation 5. Facts are fixed.	1. Depends on process, change, evolution, interconnection of experience. 2. Things are imperfectly known. 3. The nature of things is never fully grasped.

[15] Most of these are summaries from the book: Iain McGilchrist, *The Master and His Emissary* (Hobbs the Printer Ltd.; 2009).

Hemisphere	Left	Right
Effect of legions/ stroke[16]	A. Has difficulty letting go of a task. B. Can draw only two dimensions C. Figures become simplified	A. Lack of details B. Can draw 3 dimensions C. Trouble speaking

I hope you can see that we need both hemispheres in order to fully understand the world around us. We can't get along very well with reality, if we just depend on one or the other. Our goal is to use both sides of our brains effectively. Unfortunately, some people just rely and trust only one hemisphere or the other. And that is the problem. In our 'modern' American culture many people have decided to trust the world as perceived by our left-brain. And one of the results of this trust is A/NT.

When you are studying for an exam or getting ready for an interview, you are relying on the talents of your left brain. You are cramming information in the form of lists, details, flow charts and other linear forms of information into you head. You are looking for certainty and facts you will need for the exam or interview. Your right brain is not being used very much and you are basically putting it in idle while you 'crunch' the numbers and memorize the facts. Of course, this is all well and good as long as you don't continue to let your right-brain be idle and not allow it to 'digest' the information so it can become a part of you once the exam or interview is over. Unfortunately, since the left-brain is so efficient at this type of information use, many people just continue to rely on its skills and ignore the skills of the right brain. "Well, (they say to themselves) this worked well for my exam/interview, so why not use it all the time?" And that is why our society favors the left brain thinking: use and efficiency (see chart above).

[16] These effects were studied as a result of callosomy – the surgical splitting of the corpus callosum, resulting in the patient's brain not being able to communicate between hemispheres. This was done in the 1950-60s. It is no longer done.

We continually ask: "How can I use this information?" "How is this information relevant to my job, or task at hand, or keeping me healthy." "We all need to be well informed and know the 'facts.'" And these are all left-brain questions. But when do we take the time to 'digest' the information? To allow words to become a part of us? To ruminate over meaning, metaphor and paradox? To allow our right brain time to see the forest and the trees? To integrate the information, we daily receive into a unified whole, so that we actually can see patterns of thought and the connectiveness of the world around us? When we use our whole brain, we begin to 'see for real.' The world around us is not 'just one thing after another!' It is an integrated whole and highly relational. We just don't take the thought time to 'see' it. What we have become very good at recently, is becoming more and more BUSY. Now we can spend all of your days 'posting' on various social media, or texting, or e-mailing, or watching meaningless videos, playing video games; doing anything but taking time to think and 'digest' the information we have received all day long. We take little, if any time to reflect on our day.

Our lust for information that is useful has led us down the path of thought that leads us to seek the opinions of 'experts' to tell us how to use this information to better our busy lives by simplification, technology or 'facts' that help us bring order to our lives. The problem is that we don't live our lives by information, we live them by relationships. We can use information to improve our relationships and not the other way around. Again, the universe is relational, an interconnected whole. No man/woman is an island unto her/himself.

If you look at the history of philosophy, you will see the relationship between the left and right brain hemispheres. Philosophy started out in wonder, ambiguities and puzzlements with what life was all about. There was a lot of uncertainty. Then this uncertainty was unpacked, inspected from all angles, dissected and put in linear thought (logic) by the skill set of the left brain.

But philosophy realized that this every linearity of thought must be transcended, and once more left behind. This way of whole brain thinking; started with wonder and uncertainty or the right brain world, then the left brain makes it as linear as possible to understand, and then the right brain 'sees' there is much more to be known and needs to be transcended.

"Deep calls to deep.[17]" Depth is the sense of something lying beyond. We live in a technological world of pictures on flat surfaces (cell phone screens, computer screens) and these pictures have no depth. They are pixels pulled from 'reality' that they represent. And this changes the reality of existence. These pictures are decontextualized from 'reality.' If we believe they are 'reality,' we are only fooling ourselves. The 'real' event, from which we only see the picture is much more complex and nuanced than the pictures we stare at on our screens. These pictures are left brain representations of the 'real' world.

How does the brain handle false logic? Well, here is an example[18]. Take this syllogism: A) All monkeys climb trees. B) the porcupine is a monkey. Therefore, porcupines can climb trees.[19] Each brain hemisphere (right/left) has its own way of solving this logic. The left brain insists on what the written word says is true, regardless of experience, as if to say; "it says so right here." The right brain is able to see the error in the syllogism. Now, think of the people you know that insist that 'if it says so in the __________ (some authoritative text) it must be true." And that type of thinking shows how some people rely on their left brains to interpret their world. Or you might have heard the saying: "Don't confuse me with the facts, my mind is already made up." This is why I like to look at my right brain as my 'liar detection system.' A good

[17] Ps 42:7a NIV

[18] Taken from Deglin & Kinsborne, "Divergent Thinking Styles of The Two Hemispheres," Brain and Cognition vol. 31, Issue 3, August 1996.

[19] There is a porcupine in Asia that does climb trees, but the people in this study did not know of it.

metaphor to bring up at this point is how the two hemispheres of our brains working together are like a book. A book on a shelf is a self-contained object, that contains the decontextualized material that the author(s) thought important enough to write down. As long as it sits on the shelf it is lifeless, and meaningless. Only when we read the book does it come to life. As we read the book it enters our mental world where nothing is static or decontextualized. We sort through the meanings in the book and put its knowledge into the framework of our thought. So, now the book has life in us. The book in this metaphor represents the way the left brain organizes the world for our use and reading the book, represents how the right brain represents the world. It is only when they work together; book/reading, that they become meaningful.

E. Peterson, in his book on spiritual reading,[20]describes the difference between the left and right brain thinking patterns, and I don't think he even knows that he is doing it. He wrote: "Barth[21] brought it [the Bible] out of the academic mothballs in which it had been stored for so long, for so many. He demonstrated how presently alive it is, and how different it is from books that can be 'handled'- dissected and analyzed and then used for whatever we want them for. He showed clearly and persuasively, that this 'different' kind of writing *(revelatory and intimate instead of informational and impersonal)* must be met by a different kind of reading *(receptive and leisurely rather than standoffish and efficient)*." Note my use of italics. Each pair of descriptors is describing right/left brain reasoning! And for me, this gets at one of my 'pet peeves' about the use of the Bible. The Bible is not a science book! It is not informational, it is revelatory.

Have you ever wondered why men like Jesus, the Buddha and Socrates never wrote anything down? Does that seem 'logical'

---

[20] E. Peterson, *Eat This Book,* (Eerdmans Publishing Co. 2006), p.6.

[21] Karl Barth, a Swiss reformed theologian; 1886-1968; often regarded as the greatest Protestant theologian of the 20th century.

to you? Wouldn't you think that particularly Jesus should have written down his thoughts, so that now there would be no debate over the accuracy and validity of the Bible? Think about it. N. Frye wrote: "The ability to record has a lot more to do with forgetting than remembering: with keeping the past in the past, instead of continuously recreating it in the present."[22] Today, our society takes 'pics' of everything. You see people recording all their life events on Facebook, or on their phones, or with their video cameras. You can't go anywhere these days and not see people 'recording' events. Can you imagine how many 'pics' exist on cell phones? I think the number would exceed your wildest expectations. This is what a left-brain dominant society does. The belief is that if we 'record' everything we don't have to remember it and we have a 'record' of our lives to learn from. In a mere 100 years, where will all these 'pics' and videos and 'clips' be? My answer: GONE. Over 99% of them will be gone, or not remembered that they even exist. Certainly a few will be preserved in archives for future generations. But certainly not mine and very likely not yours. As our children 'sort' through our 'stuff' after our deaths, what will they preserve of our lives to be remembered? What will our great-grandchildren preserve of our lives to be remembered? And the number of 'remembrances' will decrease even more over time. Also, how many times have you looked at the video of your wedding or baptism or whatever? All these 'remembrances' are not reality. These are representations of reality.

This is the myth of left-brain thinking. If we can isolate events and study them, we have a record to learn from. So, if we decontextualize our lives in 'recordings,' we have proof of our existence and the way things were in our times. So far, how well has that worked? Are we any better at loving each other than we were 500 years ago? Are we any better at keeping the world a safe

[22] N. Frye, *The Great Code: The Bible and Literature* (Houghton Mifflin Harcourt Publishing Co. 1982) p.22

place to live in than we were 500 years ago? You're not going to like your answer.

Persons like Jesus and Buddha and Socrates knew something that we have forgotten in our left-brain world: life events are part of a flow, a continuous stream of living truths that are best remembered by lived lives, not by cell phones and cameras. In particular, Jesus was the living TRUTH. How can you write that down and take it out of the context in which it was? You can't.

Now, don't get me wrong. I think we are very lucky to have the written text we call the Bible or the other written texts about Socrates or Buddha. They are indicators for us of what these persons were like. But the texts about them are not them. Just like the map is not the territory we are in. The text only serves as a guide. It is not itself the TRUTH about these persons. So how do we get at this 'higher truth?' Keep reading for clues.

CHAPTER I
SOURCES OF ASSUMPTIONS

Context Neglect

What is 'context?' A good definition is: the set of circumstances or facts that surround a particular event, situation, etc. Notice the words 'surround' and etc. These mean to me that context involves all the 'stuff' that doesn't stand out around what we pay attention to. This brings me to the idea in perception known as 'figure-ground.' Below is a picture of a vase, or is it two people facing each other? Do you see both or only just one interpretation of the picture?

Which is the actual 'figure' and which is the actual 'ground?' or to put it another way; which image is the 'real' one? Confused? To me, the answer is both. It depends on how I see the 'figure' and how I see the 'ground.' The black part can be the context and the white part is what I pay attention to, so it is the figure or in this case the vase. But I can reverse this in my mind and see the two faces as the 'figure' and the white part as the background or context. But, before I move on, let's look at another famous 'figure;' the Necker Cube.

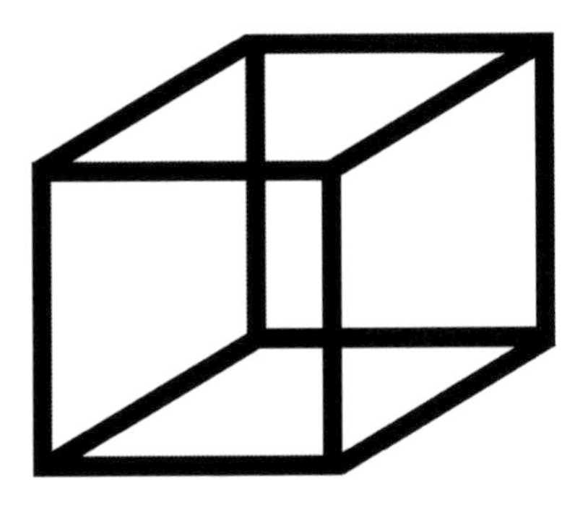

This is sometimes called the reversing cube. If you stare at it, it will seem to reverse itself and the more you stare at it the more it does this reversal. It can get a little disorienting. What I am trying to get at is that there are more ways to look at 'things' then just one, in a given situation or event. And this is what causes a lot of confusion when we take things out of their natural 'context' and assume that we know them. This is what I call context neglect. We focus on the thing we are paying attention to and ignore the 'context' in which this thing or event is embedded. I like the word embedded, because it is a good way to describe 'context.' Real knowledge comes about when we pay attention not only to the object of our attention, but also the 'context' it is embedded in. This not paying attention to 'context' is what our left-brain likes to do. Why? Because this way our left-brain can isolate a 'fact' and study it. And then our left-brain can continue to build 'fact' upon 'fact' until it comes up with a theory, even a theory of everything or as the physicists like to call it; The Grand Unified Field Theory (GUT). When we lose our sense of wonder at the world around us, we have succumbed to 'context neglect.' As Wiggenstein[1] said: "Man has to awaken to wonder... since science is a way of putting him to sleep again.[2]"

In my way of thinking this 'context neglect' is what is getting our society into with a lot of A/NT. We erroneously conclude that we have something 'figured out,' when we are neglecting the context of an event or thing to which we are giving our attention. In a larger sense, every object in the universe is embedded in the universe. Every event and object in the universe has a context and flows through time. Change is constant. We can't really isolate anything from its context in time and space. And that's the problem. (Yes, I know I am using A/NT statement, but I can't think of any exceptions.) What this means to me is that the universe is highly relational. We can't really take something out of its context and expect to fully 'know' it.

When a society relies on decontextualized pieces of information in the form of video clips, pics, text messages, online website choices, etc., to 'track' a person or decide what is going on in that person's mind by the pattern that these decontextualized pieces of information provide for the group that is 'mining the data,'[3] then we have a situation where assumptions about a person become 'facts.' These 'facts' are based on a web of decontextualized information that may or not be 'true.' But when you look at the web of information that has been achieved by this 'data mining' it looks very impressive and fools the left-brain into thinking it has this person 'all figured out.' And there is that A/NT term again; 'all.' This is Big Brother.[4] And they already exist in the Western World.

---

[1] An Austrian-British philosopher of logic

[2] http://justgreatthought.blogspot.com/2013/08/ludwig-wittgenstein-1899-1951.html (public domain)

[3] Data mining: the process of discovering patterns in large data sets involving methods (algorithms) at the intersection of machine learning (AI), statistics, and database systems.

[4] A fictional character and symbol in Orwell's *Nineteen Eighty-Four*; he is the leader of a totalitarian state.

Almost 90 year ago, Justice Brandeis[5] said: "Ways may someday be developed, by which government, without removing papers from secret drawers, can reproduce them in court, and by which it will be enabled to expose to a jury the most innocent occurrences."[6] Well, those ways have been developed. The danger is in how many assumptions they engender. When you combine this web of information and our ability to confabulate, the number of assumptions that you can make is getting worse and not better by 'data mining.'

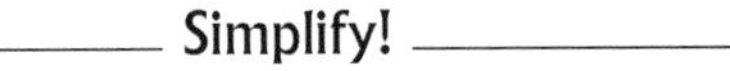

Simplify!

Life is very complicated. Life is very difficult. These two statements I have found to be true in my life of ¾ of a century. It is reasonable to 'assume' that our mind/brain is constantly looking for ways to 'simplify' this morass of existence. If we happen upon ideas that help us simplify things, then it is understandable that we will snatch it up with gusto! But beware, this comes with a price of falling into AN/T.

We have numerous books on how to simplify your life and there is a TV series called "The Simple Life." If you Google the terms simple or simplify, you will be surprised how many things come up. We humans seem to be enamored with simplifying our lives. Henry Thoreau coined this idea in his famous book "Walden" he encouraged us to 'simplify' our lives. We have coffee mugs with 'simplify' on them and all kinds of commercial products to help us 'simplify' our lives. Are you ready for a different way to look at this? Here goes: Life is NOT simple. NO 'thing' is simple. Simplicity is a myth. A better term for me would be 'streamline.' You can streamline your life, and routines, but don't 'assume' them to be simple. And you're thinking needs to be complex, not simple. In

[5] Justice of the Supreme Court of the USA from 1916-1939.

[6] Dissenting opinion in Olmstead v. United States; 1928.

fact, if you study the 'simplest' of thinking (moving your arm) you will find it very complex in what is required to do it. The 'simplest' atom (hydrogen) in the universe requires a very complex equation to describe it. Atoms are not simple at all.

I hope you can 'see' by now that when we 'simplify' our thinking we are prone to A/NT. We want to lump things and people into categories so we can deal with them more 'simply.' WARNING: Lumping anyone into a category is dangerous. Look for the things in people that make them like you not different than you.

The word 'simple' has two meanings. 1) not complex; 2) occurring or considered alone. Now hold on, no one ever explained the second one to me. In the sense of 2) above, you could consider that God is simple, since I AM is ONE (alone not lonely). God is one and God is unique. Therefore, God is simple. Never thought of it like this before, well neither did I. This is the problem we get into when we use 'simple' terms with 'simple' definitions. We limit our thinking. In the 'Christian' community this happens all the time with simple definitions for 'judgement' and 'justice' and 'love' and 'faith.' So, if we are talking about 'things' in the universe (matter and energy), there is no 'thing' that is simple. If we are talking about ideas or information, then some could be 'simple' and some 'complex,' depending on how certain we are of the idea or piece of information. For example: 2 + 2 = 4. A 'simple' idea. And that 'simple' idea has good verification in 'reality.' Ask any three-year-old. The thinking problem comes in when you decide which way to think about different ideas: 'simply' or 'complexly.'

Take for example the use of passwords for our 'sensitive' information on the internet. What are the top 10 passwords people use? The first four are: 1234, baseball, 12345678 and football. Really? Is this something we want to think about 'simply' or 'complexly?' So, then, why do people use such 'simple' passwords? I think the answer is laziness. Most people don't want to be bothered with the hard work of thinking up a complex password, much less remembering it, or even writing it down and keeping it in a safe place.

Various famous people, including Einstein have been credited with a variation of the following: *Keep 'things' as simple as possible, but no simpler.* But in reality, no 'thing' made of matter or energy in the universe, is really 'simple.' I think what Einstein and others are saying is that we need to streamline our world as much as possible so that we can get its meaning. This idea relates to a concept in science know as Occam's Razor. This is a principle of logic that says if you have competing answers to a problem, one should select the answer that makes the fewest assumptions. What do you know, just what I am trying to do- reducing the assumptions we make in our daily thinking patterns.

Now is a good time to bring the ideas of propaganda.[7] If you look through this list of propaganda techniques, you will see there is a lot of dependence on these techniques to trap someone's thinking into an A/NT style, or use ET. There are also a lot of propaganda techniques that exploit our need to 'simplify' our thinking. For example: slogans, glittering generalities, dictate, bandwagon, black and white fallacy, conditioning, and the big one; unstated assumption.

I believe that if the people in our country, or any country, would understand these propaganda techniques and become better at recognizing them, we would have a significant ability to elect honest people to our government(s). Politicians seem to me to be the people most prone to use these propaganda techniques to get your vote or convince you they are right. And then advertising would be number two on my list of propaganda sources. Many major businesses use what is now called 'behavioral economics' to get us to buy things. This 'science' of 'behavioral economics' uses such ideas as the 'halo effect,'[8] or our need for 'psychological

[7] **See Appendix I. I would highly recommend you look it over now.**

[8] A cognitive bias based on how attractive or unattractive we find a person or thing to be. These persons/things are seen with a halo over the head, or glow around them, hence the term 'halo effect.' It seems to work both positively and negatively.

symmetry' or to reduce or 'psychological pain.' This 'science' then couches these techniques into an umbrella term known as 'choice architecture.' Wow! I get confused just writing them down.

I hope you can see that these propaganda techniques are a big part of our need to simplify and make our lives 'easier' by reducing our ability to think for ourselves.

During the 2016 election cycle, a candidate from Texas said that another candidate from New York had 'New York values' (whatever that means)[9]. This term 'New York values' turns out to be a loaded term. New Yorker's immediately take offense. The candidate from Texas did not see the cultural land mine that was in front of him. His 'Texas values' got in the way (whatever that means). Now politics is a war of words; with one candidate's talking points attempting to explain the candidates 'platform' or political agenda. Each candidate has to be careful not to step on a 'political land mine'. These 'landmines' can be cultural or taboo politically. The problem is that if a candidate is prone to simplistic thinking (like most of us) he/she will explode one of these mines and very often does not know that one is right in front of them. Is there not a school for candidates, particularly on the national stage, where they can learn where and how these landmines are placed on the political landscape? I think it would be most helpful to them. If I were teaching such a course, I would start with one rule that is engaged before a candidate says anything, "Pause, and think about what you are about to say." I have seen some candidates do that, and they generally don't commit this kind of error in speech. Then when the Texas candidate tried to explain what that meant, it only got worse. The best approach (and this is usually true) is to apologize. "My bad. I wasn't thinking clearly." Now that's closer to the truth.

Here is what I think is the thinking problem: We are each 'brought up' in a region of the USA and in a state in the USA and

[9] The candidate's names are not important in my argument.

this can cause problems in our thinking. Most of the time if you travel around the USA you find that you can generalize about a region, or a state. This is not a good idea, and I am not sure it is valid one to do. And we all have learned about 'Southerners' and 'Midwesterners' and 'Northerners' and 'Those people in California', and on and on the list goes. The reality is that each state and each 'region' of the USA is made up of individuals with individual values and interests and preferences. There may exist a 'generalized' value of preference for each state and/or region, but that is not the job of a candidate for a national office. He/she 'should' represent the values of the country. The good old' USA. Fortunately, we have two documents that explain some of our values. Those documents are The Constitution of the United States and The Declaration of Independence. A civil war was fought over what these documents mean and today there continues battles over what they mean in our Congress and in our Supreme Court. "We hold these truths to be self-evident," and hopefully all Americans know what those 'truths' are. This is the arena where politics hold debate, not on Texas values, or New York values but American Values.

Again, the problem is in how we think. We are so prone to simplification, that it can come back and bite us in our Texas behind, or our New York behind, or whatever state behind you have.

In their book about the Holy Spirit, Hauerwas and Willimon say "Most heresies are attempts to simplify beliefs about God."[10] Here we are again in the realm of 'simplicity.' How is it possible to simplify the most complex 'thing' you can conceive of; God? What is the motive of people who wish to 'simplify' God? In my way of thinking it is to contain God in some way. To make Him/She/It, a controllable 'thing.' To take a dynamic and make I AM static, so we can 'know' IT better. And doesn't everyone want to

[10] S. Hauerwas & W.H. Willimon, *The Holy Spirit,* (Abington Press, 2015) p.4.

'know' God better? Of course. But God is a true paradox.[11] But God, knew our dilemma and sent a Person (Jesus the human-God) to give us a better picture of what I AM was like. And then this Jesus sent us another 'equal' part of God called the 'Paraclete'[12] (Spirit). Now things get really complex. In order to contain what is very complex, we have come up with ideas of how to simplify this three-part God (Trinity). But even those attempts cause heresies and misunderstandings about the nature of God. What's a God believer to do?

As I have said before, we live in a left-brain society that likes to decontextualize things so we can 'study' them and 'know' them better. So, when we have a 'spiritual experience,' we chalk it up to some irregularity in our mood, or diet, or circumstances. We file it away as a strange, but interesting event in our lives. After all we want to make our lives 'simpler' and not more complex. In my experience, 'spiritual experiences' are all around us, we just need to attend to their reality. In other words, pay attention to the undefined world around us every day. Let it be. Let it be what it is. Let the Holy Other speak to us through the natural world around us.[13]

When the universe began around 13.6 billion years ago, it was all hydrogen atoms. A fairly 'simple' system. But over the last 13.6 billion years the universe we know, became more and more complex. Now we have 98 naturally occurring elements of which hydrogen is only one. Organic compounds[14] are now found among inorganic compounds across the universe. Life began, and

---

[11] Read my section on paradox; p.27

[12] Greek for advocate or helper (Holy Spirit in the New Testament).

[13] See Ro 1:19-20 NIV. I particularly like version in the Message.

[14] Any compound containing the element carbon, but more strictly having a carbon-hydrogen bond. Estimates of the number of organic vs inorganic compounds are; 500,000 inorganic to 4,000,000 organic compounds; 8 times more organic compounds, because of the vast array of possibilities for carbon bonds.

the 'simple cell' formed. The 'simple cell' is anything but simple. Just begin reading any book on the cell. The universe has reached a state of complexity unknown until now. Then add on the idea of consciousness. How much more complex is that? And where did it come from? Animals have it. Maybe plants have it. We have it. But our consciousness is even more complex. We have self-consciousness. We can observe ourselves and criticize ourselves and change our behaviors and how we think. We can examine ourselves and self-reflect. Us humans are the most complex organisms of all, so far. And we are the only organisms on this planet capable of knowing about another 'reality'. The 'reality' of the metaphysical[15]. The Other (God). We are the only worshipping animal. There really is no such thing as 'the simple life,' only those who yearn for it.

Another idea that helps with understanding the myth of 'simplicity' is the fact that we live in an open universe and not a closed one. What does this mean? The universe we live in has a time direction. We move from past to future. How God relates to this time direction that we all perceive I have written about later in this book. You might want to go there now and read it to better understand what I am going to say. There is a process in the universe that science calls entropy. Entropy is a process where everything is moving in time from states of more complex to states of less complex. Energy is dissipating and matter is changing to 'simpler' states over time. And that is a streamlined definition for me. This is called 'time's arrow' (past to future). Entropy shows that this direction is happening. Things rust. Things decay. "for dust you are, and to dust you will return."[16] The universe is gradually running down. This is called the 'heat death' of the universe. But what is it that has been providing this increase in complexity

[15] Metaphysics: the underlying principles of a subject or field of inquiry: ontology, cosmology.

[16] Ge 3:19b NIV

of life on this planet? It is the sun. The sun has provided all the energy necessary for the creation/evolution of life over the last 4.6 billion years and it will provide energy for life for the foreseeable future.[17] My point is this: The created universe is extremely complex because of the capture of energy by stars on planets like ours. But all this energy that the sun sends us each day, most of it is dissipated (entropy) into space![18] So, if you imagine all the stars and all the available energy in the universe being dissipated (and you and I can't) you get the idea that entropy is happening. Not very simple!!

Another part of the myth of simplicity is not knowing the difference between a sign and a symbol. Or if some 'thing' is both. Back to the dictionary. A sign is any object, action, event, pattern, etc., that conveys meaning. Like a stop sign, or a cross, or a sign of the Zodiac. A symbol is something used for or regarded as **representing something else**. The key to the difference is that a symbol is a representation of something else. Like a letter of the alphabet, or a chemical symbol like Cu for copper, or x in algebra for an unknown quantity. Also, a word is a combination of symbols that is a sign for something else. A sign is more complicated and more complex being more in the realm of an event, or pattern as described in its definition. A sign is made up more than one symbol to convey a meaning. Unfortunately, the terms sign and symbol are many times used interchangeably in our culture and it is hard to get the meaning when this happens.

Generally, I think, we give signs more of our attention than symbols. Take the symbol 'c.' Now just that letter alone doesn't cause you to contemplate what it means, but if you use it in an equation like $E= mc^2$, now the 'c' has meaning, in this case the speed of light. Is the symbol 'c' now a sign? I think so, because it conveys meaning. But it has to be in a group of symbols that alone

---

[17] Estimates are another 5 billion years.

[18] Over 50 percent. A good estimate.

do not convey meaning, but together they do. Confusing, isn't it. So, in my way of thinking a symbol is like a place holder that only contains meaning when connected to other symbols, like a word or a chemical formula or equation. For example: Look at this string of letters: LSDN BCT VF BIU SA. Do they make sense? Well, what if I rearrange them to: LSD NBC TV FBI USA. Now do they? How I place them together makes a lot of difference. So, for me, a word, or acronym is a sign and a sentence is a more complex sign, and a paragraph even more complex, and so on. It sure isn't simple is it?

Metaphors

Here is a word that is very important as a thinking tool. First, as usual, let's get a good definition. A metaphor is in the realm of analogies. Analogies are thinking tools to compare one subject to another, to put it 'simply.' What makes a metaphor different is that a metaphor compares two things based on similarities that you may not have 'seen' between the two things being compared. A classic example is from Shakespeare: "All the world's a stage."[19] The world is not really a stage, but a lot of the time people behave as if it was. In other words, people in the social world don't really show each other themselves, but 'act' and hide who they really are or protect themselves out of distrust for the social world around them. A two-year-old learns this lesson when they learn to lie to their parents, in order to get what they want.

A metaphor is a way to 'carry' (phor; Greek: pherein) our thinking 'across' (Greek: meta) one way of thinking to another. It can be said that a metaphor causes us to use both sides of our brain instead of just the right or left hemisphere. As noted before, we tend to be a left-brain thinking society and a metaphor is a way to get us to use our whole brain. Metaphors are used to bring together the 'whole' of one thing to the 'whole' of another thing

[19] From Shakespeare's play; "As You Like It."

so that each is looked at in a different perspective. Jesus used a lot of metaphors in his teachings about the Kingdom of God and obeying his commands. In the Sermon on the Mount[20] Jesus says that following his commands is like building your house on a rock. He doesn't mean that his commands are literally rocks. But the metaphor of commands and rocks communicate solidity. Both are solid ways to practice life. You live your life on the commands of God (rock) and not on the world's way to live your life (buying all you can, hating your enemies, getting even, etc.).

The problem with metaphors is that our left-brained society doesn't like them. They are two 'uncertain' to be useful. Our left-brained society likes certainty and 'facts,' one at a time so that it can build up its theories and laws in a dependable way. Eventually having everything figured out this way.

Metaphors are 'literally'[21] lies. For example: In a lot of the parables of Jesus, He compares the Kingdom of God to many things; a pearl of great price, a mustard seed, sowing seeds, a net, a king settling accounts, or hiring men to work in a vineyard. These are all meant as a way of comparison. And none of them are the Kingdom of God. But each of these things; pearl, seed, hiring people, etc. are 'how' the Kingdom of God works.

If you read John 6:30-66, you will find a changing metaphor. This is the section where Jesus describes himself as "the bread of life." Many people read this passage and think: 'yes, Jesus is the bread of life and this is why we take bread at communion to symbolize this idea.' But Jesus takes this metaphor further and connects the manna (bread), that God provided to the Hebrews during the Exodus, to Himself. This causes great confusion in his listeners. Jesus then adds that He is the bread (manna) that came down from heaven and further adds more confusion by saying that we need to eat his flesh and drink his blood. Wow! Talk

---

[20] Mt 7: 24-27 NIV

[21] In this sense 'literally' means if you look at a metaphor in its factual sense.

about shifting metaphors. Jesus takes this to a very disagreeable level. At this point many who 'believed' in Him, left Him. Jesus then in effect says that even if I ascended back to heaven, would that convince you I am the bread come down from heaven? Then Jesus gives a little explanation. The 'words' He spoke are "full of Spirit[22]" and the "flesh counts for nothing.[23]" In other words, this is a spiritual concept, not a literal one! This whole spiritual idea is a way for Jesus to see who his 'real' disciples are.

If you have noticed in your life, you run into people who take most of what you tell them literally and don't get the analogy or metaphors that you are using. Puns are based on this type of thinking, where you compare something in a way that was not seen before, and the sudden change in meaning is funny (but not to everyone). I have two sons. One loves puns and one doesn't like them at all. When my pun loving son and I go on a pun fest, and we are with his brother, all his brother does is roll his eyes and tell us how 'silly' we are. I have found that people who enjoy puns usually have a good ability to understand metaphor.

The Bible is shock full of metaphors, so if you are reading it with only your left-brain, you will quickly get very confused. As E. Peterson says: "If we don't understand how metaphor works we will misunderstand most of what we read in the Bible. No matter how carefully we parse our Hebrew and Greek sentences, no matter how carefully we use our dictionaries and trace our etymologies, no matter how exactly we define the words on the page, if we do not appreciate the way a metaphor works we will never comprehend the meaning of the text."[24] And that is the 'beauty' of a metaphor, it communicates on a much deeper level of thinking. Metaphors help us 'see' the higher truths in life.

One of my friends has put a sizable amount of money in zero

[22] Jn 6:63 NIV

[23] Jn 6:63 NIV

[24] E. Peterson, *Eat This Book,* (Eerdman's Publishing Co. 2006) p.93. (Peterson is the guy who is responsible for *The Message*)

interest US Treasury bonds (Yes, zero interest). He based this decision on a book he read by a man who claimed he could predict the stock market. His predictions were based on an idea called the Fibonacci sequence.[25] The interesting part to me is that this sequence has been used in art, science and mysticism. The ratio developed from this sequence, known as the 'golden ratio' has been found in nature, used in art, and equated with the dimensions of the cross of Jesus the Christ. We really don't know what the cross of Jesus the Christ looked like. There is no description of it in the Bible. To me, it doesn't make any difference anyway. But to be able to predict something as highly unpredictable as the stock market is in my mind is quite a stretch of my thinking. And as my friend put his money in this 'system' of stock market prediction, I noticed that the author of this prediction system had to revise his stock market 'forecast' several times. Hmm. This is the danger of using a mathematical metaphor such as the Fibonacci sequence as a predictor. A metaphor is for finding deeper meaning, not prediction.

Parables are a story form for a metaphor. As you may remember a metaphor is best understood by your right brain. A parable allows us to reconnect to a world that is flowing and relational, not fixed and decontextualized. A parable attempts to allow the connections between our left and right brains to communicate, so that we can find more layers of meaning within the parable. It is only when both sides of our brain are working in harmony, do we see the deeper meanings in a parable. Jesus used parables a lot. If you read some of His more famous ones, like the sower, the weeds, talents, the shrewd manager, and a lot on lost things like, a sheep, a coin or a son. Most of the parables of Jesus can be found in two of the books of the New Testament: Matthew and Luke.

---

[25] A sequence where every number after the first two is a sum of the two preceding numbers. This was found in Indian mathematics and the "Liber Abaci" by Leonardo Fibonacci (1202). Goggle the 'golden ratio' and you will be amazed at what you find.

And after some of the parables Jesus makes a curious statement: "Though seeing, they do not see, though hearing, they do not hear or understand."[26] It seems that two of His more famous parables, the sower and the weeds, his disciples don't 'get it.' They ask him to explain the parables. My take on this is that the disciples were just using their left brains and not using their whole brains when Jesus told these parables. It seems there was a lot of left-brain thinkers even two thousand years ago. The Bible does not tell us whether the disciples then understood the parables after Jesus explained them. I like to think they did.

So, it seems, Jesus had a lot of trouble explaining spiritual ideas to His generation, particularly the Pharisees, who seem to be very left brained, interpreting the Torah for their purely utilitarian purposes (making money was one). Even our 'Christian' churches today try to appeal to the left brainers by attempting to reduce the Gospel down to such ideas like 'steps to salvation' and a 'catalogue of sins,' or demonstrating the 'certainty' of belief in God, as if God is something to be proven like a geometry problem. All of these attempts to decontextualize spiritual ideas get lost in the process of trying to pin them down to physical constructs. The Spirit is life and flow and relationship. It refuses to be 'pinned down' with 'facts.'

Confabulation

Which brings me to the concept of confabulate[27]. This word comes to us from the French for 'chatting together' and in psychology the term means: 'fabricating information for gaps in memory.' Now this is where I want to concentrate: fabricating information as a result of gaps in our memory. When the brain is asked to retrieve

[26] Mt 13:13 and 43. NIV Also verses 34-35 are instructive about parables. In these verses Matthew relates parables to mysteries (see book section on mystery).
[27] For a great example, see January, 2018 issue of Smithsonian Magazine regarding who took the 'earthrise' picture from the Apollo Spacecraft in 1968.

information about us, like our phone number or address, we have used that neural path so often that it has no problem accurately giving us the information we seek. However, when it is asked to retrieve information that is used infrequently, it has trouble, so it supplies the nearest item it can recall, that is closest to the information requested. This is the process of confabulation. It seems our brains hate incompleteness. This is not, and I repeat, not lying. This is an important point, since our facility to confabulate is an 'unconscious' process, rather than a deliberate process to hide the truth either overtly or covertly. The next point is that over time these confabulations (if repeated often enough, or often discussed), get consolidated into a memory network. Gradually the original memory is transformed and encoded into a considerably different one that we believe to be true and accurate. This is why law enforcement finds 'witness' memories to be so inconsistent and unreliable. Many experiments in this area have confirmed how easy it is to distort a person's recollection of recent events, or even 'implant' memories[28]. When we have no ***independent verification***, it is impossible to decide what events in the recalled 'repressed memory' actually occurred and which is the result of confabulation. This is reason why it is so important to have another witness confirm our memory, or we have a system available to verify our observations. This system that we use to verify our observations we call science. This is also the reason why we need to understand the techniques of propaganda[29] and how easily the 'truth' can be manipulated by people to convince others that their beliefs are true. When we have a culture that is ignorant of either or both of these methods of verification we have a dangerous situation.

This lack of verification is where all three kinds of thinking

---

[28] E. Loftus, and K. Ketcham, *The Myth of Repressed Memory* (St. Martin's Press, 1995).

[29] See Appendix 1: In fact, you might want to read it again, now.

patterns that I have mentioned (A/NT, ET and AT) come in. Usually these thinking patterns are a result of un-verified thinking or poor assumptions being made. So, when we find leaders in a culture undermining science and or our sources of information (fake news, etc.) we have a very dangerous thinking patterns going on. If you don't know who to 'trust' or what sources of information are true, you become more confused and unable to make good decisions in thinking.

An example from my life is when a friend of mine became more and more fearful as time went by. He began to be interested in many of the 'conspiracy theories' that were becoming more and more prevalent on the internet and TV. The usual patterns in these 'conspiracy theories' is they provide some form of visual documentation to the readers/viewers and then go about using propaganda techniques to convince the readers/viewers that these visual documents are true, either through 'witnesses' and/or 'experts' that are presented as 'experts' when the reader/viewer has no way of verifying these statements. Many of the statements used in these 'conspiracy theories' in themselves are confabulations. So, my friend as time went on, began to believe these conspiracies were true and valid, when in fact they could very easily be 'debunked' if one took the time to do so. And here is where we run into the most challenging part of our thinking: 'taking the time to check out what we hear and see!' Most of us are pretty lazy when it comes to thinking and we would rather just not take the time to check things out for ourselves and it is easier to believe some 'authority' that we assume to be right.

There is a very interesting scripture in one of Paul's letters. In 1 Thessalonians, Paul states: "Prove all things; hold fast that which is good.[30]" Of course, even Paul uses A/NT in this statement, but here I can't agree that 'all' things need to be proved. There are some pretty important things that I need to know, which cannot

[30] 1 Th 1:26 NIV

be proven. But, in other words, Paul is telling us not to just believe anything we hear or see, but to seek proof. Proving things is the realm of science and we cannot get through life without knowing how to do science in our everyday life.

But science is limited in its use. Science can only deal with what are called repeatable phenomena. In other words, events we observe that happen over and over in time, so that we can learn 'how' they work. Science calls these repeatable events (phenomena) 'observations' or 'data.' This is part of what most of us learned in school called the scientific method. But what about events or phenomena that occur only once? These are called 'singularities' and one of the most well-known is the Big Bang.[31]

"Was a tiny mummy in Atacama an alien? No, but the real story is almost as strange." [32]The 'mummy' was recently given a DNA test and found to be very much human, with a considerable number of mutations causing the 'alien' like appearance. It was most likely a stillborn baby. This 'mummy' was used in a 2013 'documentary' on U.F.Os in 2013, presenting this 'mummy' as evidence for aliens coming to earth. Here is an example of how confabulation can work in your brain. Many people who saw the 'documentary on U.F.Os in 2013 used this erroneous piece of information as 'proof' that aliens had come to earth and left one of their stillborn offspring. The brain can then 'fill in' the missing information, with all the trappings of space ships and what aliens must look like, etc. And, of course, how many of those people who were fooled by this mummy will read the headline debunking their erroneous belief? Not many.

And then there is what M. S. Peck called 'bracketing.' This is putting oneself aside, silencing the familiar, and welcoming the strange and new.[33] This can be a good thing when it comes to

---

[31] You might want to read my section on singularities; p.91

[32] This is a story headline from 3/22/2018 in the NY Times by C. Zimmer.

[33] M. S. Peck, *The Road Less Traveled- 25th Anniversary Ed,* (Touchstone; division of Simon & Schuster, Inc. 2003) p.73

learning about ourselves, other people, cultures and new ideas. This can be a bad thing when we welcome the strange and new as in 'life on other planets,' or 'aliens coming to earth.' I am not arguing a premise for these ideas either way. I am pointing out how we can 'bracket' a set of bad assumptions so we can 'believe' these new ideas. Let me give an example in the idea of 'aliens coming to earth:' a) So, what if there are undiscovered elements and life on other planets are based on these elements? b) these aliens can travel faster than the speed of light. c) these aliens have superior intellect; d) and they evolved many years before us. So, the 'bracketed' mind start to add up all these 'what ifs' that are based on unknown 'facts,' until you have a belief based on only unknown assumptions. Yes, it could be true. But, is it probable? And here is where the problem in thinking lies. Rational thought can only go from what we know to be true to what is not known. Rationalizing [34] thought is thinking that goes from unknown to unknown. There is a big difference between reasoning and rationalizing. A 'bracketed mind' is what I think is causing the problem in thinking by generating too many assumptions. And this can be a form of confabulation.

Narcissism

Our American society has become more hubristic over the last 50 years. This is demonstrated by the increase in narcissism in our culture[35]. What occurs to me is the need for many of us to believe short snippets of information devoid of context. We like to believe chopped up pieces of information, either presented to us in the form of videos or acts that the videographer has edited and chopped up to allow their particular prejudices to be displayed as 'truth;' when the context of what they have 'taped' is only part of

[34] Rationalize – to invent plausible explanations for acts, opinions, etc., that are actually based on other causes.

[35] Elizabeth Lunbeck, *The Americanization of Narcissism,* (by Elizabeth Lunbeck, 2014).

the context of what actually occurred. There are many examples of this going on every day. These are 'platforms' for narcissism to show itself in our culture, as each person strives to get his/her 15 minutes of fame to massage their egos. This is why social media sources such as Twitter, Snapchat, U-Tube and Instagram have become so prevalent. The danger of such 'decontextualized' pieces of information is that they are first of all believed as 'true' and secondly, they reinforce some virulent A/NT thinking.

A good example of what I mean was demonstrated on July 4th 2017. National Public Radio (NPR) 'tweeted' the Declaration of Independence by chopping it up into segments (they could only use 140 characters at a time) and presenting it as these chopped up segments. Headlines read: "NPR tweets Declaration of Independence and people freak out about a 'revolution.'[36]" Many people did not recognize the Declaration of Independence in this context and even went so far as to say things on Twitter as: "NPR is inciting revolution and should be defunded." This is a great example of what happens when we 'decontextualize' events, documents and sources. What were they thinking? They weren't. The point is not many people in this incident were 'thinking.'

What it seems that many of us have lost our ability to do is 'self-reflect' on what we have observed in our environment. I think 'self-reflection' is a lost pattern of thinking in our narcissistic culture. Just what do I mean by 'self-reflection?' Let me start with a very old and good mind: Socrates, the Greek philosopher. He said (or is attributed to him): "An unexamined life is not worth living." Well that gets us started. When we go around just reacting to things from our inflated egos (like the example above) we haven't used our ability to 'self-reflect.'

I think that 'self-reflection' involves three steps. 1) we observe a piece of information (video, Tweet, picture, etc.) that is taken out of the flow of life. 2) We react to what we see or hear. 3) We send

---

[36] Kansas City Star; July 5th 2017

our reaction back to our brain for a context or frame of reference to what we observed. It seems that a lot of us don't do step three. We just react without examining our observation of a piece of information. In other words, we jump to a conclusion. Here we are again, leaping into A/NT.

And before I forget to mention; we are all narcissistic to some extent. We all jump to conclusions at times, sometimes more, sometimes less.

Now, how about a definition of narcissism we can work with. Narcissism: excessive self-love; vanity. The word to focus on in this definition is EXCESSIVE. Now that's the problem; a little self-love, goes a long way, but excessive self-love leads to another thing called arrogance.[37] There have been many studies done on the relationship of narcissism to arrogance,[38] and most of the time you will see these two terms linked. So narcissistic people tend to be arrogant people. The arrogance you observe is just the symptom of the excessive self-love. Another term that we seem to get mixed up in this area is PRIDE. And again, there are different forms that pride can take. C. S. Lewis said that 'pride' was "The Great Sin.[39]" Nowadays we don't like the word 'sin' since we think it is an 'archaic' term and should be replaced. But that is another issue. Lewis goes on to say: "Unchastity [another archaic term], anger, greed, drunkenness, and all that, are mere fleabites in comparison [to pride]: it was through Pride that the devil [another archaic term] became the devil: Pride leads to every other vice: it is the complete anti-God state of mind." So, we have three terms that basically describe in varying degrees the opposite of humility; narcissism, arrogance, and pride. The umbrella term would be pride. But is there a 'good' form of pride? We say such things as "I am proud of" my daughter, or son, or whatever. I don't think that is

---

[37] Arrogance – offensive display of self-importance.

[38] Just "Goggle" the terms arrogance & narcissism and you will get a lot of articles from various sources.

[39] C. S. Lewis; *Mere Christianity,* (HarperOne, 1952; renewed 1980) p. 121

the same as pride in yourself. And also, there is a needed measure of self-love that we need to keep ourselves healthy and mentally stable. Taking pleasure in being praised for something you did, or something you are, is not this EXCESSIVE form of pride, or self-love that I am referring to. As usual, what is needed in life is perspective. To see ourselves as no better or no worse than any other human being. To really believe we are more alike than we are different from each other.

And when we let our self-love rule us (narcissism), we are subject to replacing God for the holy trinity of the self; my needs, my wants, and my feelings.[40] I then start telling myself to 'think big' and 'don't settle for less' and 'you deserve this' and whatever other ad catchphrase you can think of to lure your sense of narcissism into buying a product. Even more enticing are the many self-help gurus who tell us such things as 'you are gods,'[41] which certainly doesn't help us relinquish our holy needs, wants and feelings. We are brought up in a culture that tells us to be individuals, and don't let anybody get in the way of you being 'who you are.' The problem with this is that we are constantly bumping into other beings who have been nurtured in the same way. As a result, many married couples break apart because they 'need their own space' or 'have grown apart' or have 'irreconcilable differences,' all because of the sovereignty the holy trinity of self-love.

But what happens when we have a group of narcissists together, reinforcing each other in their behavior? What happens when group pride takes over the thinking of a group and is then reinforced by their group culture and rituals? What happens when these groups start chanting slogans like: "We're number one!" or "Build the wall!" or "No more guns!" or "Abortion is evil!" or any other slogan you can think of that a group uses to make its point in society. Well, in my way of thinking you have a 'specialized' group. Dr.

---

[40] Thanks to E. Peterson, *Eat This Book,* (Eerdmans Publishing Co. 2006) p.32.

[41] Attributed to Dr. Wayne Dyer in his self-help videos.

Scott Peck talked about what a specialized group was in his book *People of The Lie*[42], which I would recommend reading for a good understanding of what human evil is all about. He said: "For the reality is that it is not only possible but easy and even natural for a large group to commit evil without emotional involvement simply by turning loose its specialists [referring to armies]. It happened in Vietnam. It happened in Nazi Germany. I am afraid it will happen again."[43] In this quote, I think what he meant by a 'specialized' group is particularly significant. Cultures around the world have 'specialized' groups known as armies, police, intelligence services, security forces, etc. They are all specialized to do a particular job, and more to my point, they develop within their ranks a sense of pride and in some cases narcissism about their 'specialized' group. And further, when this pride and/or narcissism is threatened these groups can easily become the very destructive in their response to criticism. A case in point, which is now very much removed in time and illustrates what pride and narcissism can do to a 'specialized group' is what happened during the Vietnam War.[44] America began its involvement in the Vietnam War in 1961. As our government escalated the war through the 1960's, the pride of our military was wounded significantly. And as Peck points out in People of the Lie, "... (the army) began to strike out with **uncharacteristic** viciousness and deceit against the Vietnamese people, who were wreaking such havoc on its self-esteem. Suspected spies were tortured, Viet Cong bodies, dead or perhaps still alive, were dragged in the dirt behind armored personnel carriers."[45] The word here to think about is 'uncharacteristic.' During WWII and The

[42] M. Scott Peck, People *of the Lie,* (Simon and Schuster Inc. 1983).

[43] Peck, *People of the Lie,* 232.

[44] 1955 – 1975. I bet a lot of you thought it was shorter. America's participation was about 13 years.

[45] Peck, *People of the Lie,* 236. It is interesting to note that Peck was an officer in the US Army.

Korean War, American forces were known for their enforcement of the Geneva Conventions.[46]

Then there is this thing called national pride. This is when a nation sees itself as superior to other nations as reflected in the attitudes and behavior of its people. We give this national pride various names like 'populism,' or 'egalitarianism,' and a lot of other 'isms.' I think that most of these 'isms' can be seen as a result of pride in some group philosophy that represents a people[47].

Mark Twain gives us a good example of the destructiveness of national pride in his little known short story called "The War Prayer."[48] Below is the main part of a prayer used in this story. The countries involved in the war are not named. The story takes place in a church with the people calling upon their god. This was written 5 years before his death in 1910. He had lived through the Civil War, the Spanish-American war and the Philippine-American war.

"Lord our Father, our young patriots, idols of our hearts, go forth into battle – be Thou near them! With them – in spirit- we also go forth from the sweet peace of our beloved firesides to smite the foe. O Lord our God, help us tear their soldiers to bloody shreds with our shells; help us to cover their smiling fields with the pale forms of their patriot dead; help us to drown the thunder of guns with the shrieks of their wounded, writhing in pain; help us to wring the hearts of their unoffending widows with unavailing grief; help us to turn them out roofless with their little children to wander unfriended in the wastes of their desolated land in rags and hunger and thirst, sports of the sun flames in summer and the icy

---

[46] Four treaties and protocols that establish the standards of international law for humanitarian treatment in war. 196 countries agreed to them.

[47] The entire body of persons who constitute a community, tribe, nation by their common culture.

[48] Written by Mark Twain in 1905. You can find the full text of this short story at: https://warprayer.org

winds of winter, broken is spirit, worn with travail, imploring Thee for the refuge of the grave and denied it." [excerpted]

This story was not published until long after Twain's death in 1910. Twain's family refused to do so. Twain's reply to his friend and illustrator (who wanted to publish it) is instructive: "No, I have told the whole truth in that, and only dead men can tell the truth in this world. It can be published after I am dead.[49]"

What is important to me about this 'prayer' is the shift of perspective that Twain uses. The perspective is that of what happens to the defeated foe. What the ravages of war brings to the vanquished. During the 2003 War in Iraq, the phrase 'shock and awe' was used many times and then we saw the result of the American 'shock and awe' campaign. Even many years later America still 'celebrates' the glory of American soldiers during this war. As after World War II, many movies and television shows attest to this fact.

As the centuries roll by and war after war are fought, the perspective of this "War Prayer" goes on. In 2001 America was attacked by 'terrorists' who brought the 'shock and awe' to America, the homeland. As a result, a new department in the government was created: Homeland Security. Patriotism became an American obsession as American flags appeared almost everywhere. A 'war on terrorism' was declared. And now for the first time in American history we faced an enemy with no uniform, or border to protect, and no clear ideology. But these 'terrorists' had to have a uniform, so we used the uniform of the Muslims. But these 'terrorists' had to have a border to protect, so we labeled this border as 'all Muslim countries.' But these 'terrorists' had to have an ideology, so we labeled it 'extreme Islamic terrorists,' or 'Muslim jihadists.' Now we had defined a 'clear and present danger' to America.

I hope you can see that having a narrow perspective about what it means to be a 'Proud American' or for that matter a 'Proud

---

[49] https://warprayer.org

Russian' or any other country, can take a turn into destructive thinking and behavior, when it becomes EXCESSIVE. Then it takes on the form of narcissism and arrogance. Don't get me wrong, I am proud to be an American, like I am proud of my children and grandchildren. America is a great nation, among many other great nations. Nations are great based on the unique histories that they have and the unique talents of the individuals that make up a nation. Truly great nations are the ones who can be humble among their neighboring nations.

The word humility to me is the opposite of narcissism. The word derives from the Latin for earth; hummus; but it can also mean 'grounded.' And that's the term I like best for humility. A person who is grounded in how they think about themselves. These humble people see themselves as no better or worse than any other human. They are 'down to earth.' They are 'grounded' by their sense of their relationship to God. When comparing ourselves to God, we are truly humbled.

Paradox Confusion

What is a paradox? Here is another word that gets in the way of understanding. A paradox is a statement that contains rational ideas that seem to be in contradiction to each other. For example, if I have my grandfather's axe (which consists of a handle and an axe head) and I replace over time the handle and the axe head, is it still my grandfather's axe? Or, more complex, if I have a wooden boat and I replace one by one all the pieces of the boat, after I have replaced them in time, is it the same boat I started with? If you choose to be a left-brain thinker, then you would either just say that the paradox cannot be resolved or you just ignore it.

To illustrate this problem of paradox further let's use the paradox of sand grains and sand heaps.[50] When does adding grains

[50] Sorites paradox, from the Greek for heap.

of sand together constitute a heap of sand? Well, a good scientist would say that you have to define a heap of sand. In other words, have a standard for measuring a heap of sand. A grain of sand is pretty well defined to 1. But say I define a heap of sand as 25 grains of sand. Does that make a heap for you? Have you ever put 25 grains of sand together? Does it 'look like' a heap? Some would say yes and some would say no. So, we have a problem with our defining a heap of sand. The point is our left-brain wants to believe that the whole (heap) is the sum of its parts so it tries to relate the two things: grain/heap. So, there must be either a heap or not a heap. This is known as an either/or.[51] What this implies is an obvious paradox. But there is another view. That a heap is a gradual process of becoming, a process in time, so as grains of sand are added a heap is formed at some point in time and it does not matter how many grains of sand there are, we all would 'see' a heap. A sand grain and a heap of sand are a changing thing in time[52] and when we take it out of its context (time, background) we lose some important aspects of its 'being.'

Another important idea in science is the understanding light. Is light a particle or a wave? There are properties of light which show that it is a particle (photons) and there are properties of light which show it as a wave (energy frequencies). So, which is it? I think a good answer is that it is both a particle and a wave. In their book "The Evolution of Physics,[53]" A. Einstein and L. Infeld thought that both the idea of light being a particle and a wave presented science with a new difficulty. That light can be BOTH a particle and a wave seemed contradictory. What these great men of science decided is that light must be thought of as BOTH a particle and a wave, together. The phenomenon of light is a complementarity. It is this idea of togetherness that Einstein and Infeld thought best explained light. Wow! It's a relationship! Now the left-brained

---

[51] A logical disjunction.

[52] Ever hear the metaphor 'the sands of time?'

[53] A. Einstein and L. Infeld, *The Evolution of Physics* (Simon & Schuster, 1938 copyright renewed, 1966) p. 263. This page contains their original quote.

thinker doesn't like this. "How can I study this thing called light if I don't hold it still, separate it and then find out what it is?"

I guess now is a good time to explain the idea of complementarity. Complementarity is similar to the Uncertainty Principle that I mention one page 113. This principle holds that 'objects' (in this case light) have properties which complete each other which cannot all be observed or measured simultaneously. Here again we have a relational idea. This is similar to the idea of marriage, when Jesus says: "For this reason a man will leave his father and mother and be united with his wife, and the two will become one flesh. So, they are no longer two, but one.[54]" Here we see the idea of complementarity in the scriptures. This 'thing' called a marriage is the formation of a new being; a marriage. Again, a relationship: husband and wife complete each other and they become this one 'thing' called a marriage.

So now on to the big point. It appears that the universe we live in is very relational and in order to begin to understand it we must be willing to let go of our need to examine it on our terms and understand it on its terms. We must be willing to hold two seemingly opposites together in relationship to understand it's meaning. It is in the tension of the opposites that insights occur. Many things in our world that appear to be a paradox, are in fact complementarities.

[54] Mt 19:5 NIV (Here Jesus quotes Ge 2:24 NIV)

Mystery/Miracle/Magic

Time for some operational definitions:[55]

- ***Mystery***: anything that is kept secret or remains unexplained or unknown.
- ***Miracle***: an effect or extraordinary event in the physical world that surpasses all known human or natural powers and is ascribed to a supernatural cause.[56]
- ***Magic***: the art of producing illusions as entertainment by the use of sleight of hand, deceptive devices. Also, the use of incantations or various other techniques that presumably assure human control of supernatural agencies or forces of nature.

Now for the daunting task of comparing these terms. All three terms delve into the area of the 'unknown' (supernatural, magical techniques, deception). These are areas in our thinking where we have more questions than understanding. A materialist would say: "Bah, humbug"[57] or this is pure hogwash. And they may be right. But: There are a lot of humans who have had the experience of miracles that would tell these materialists they are wrong. It is always wise not to readily discredit a first-hand account of anything.

How are these three terms different? Well, mystery tells us that we can eventually explain something that was unknown in the past but can be known in the future. A miracle is an event that we cannot explain in the present, but maybe we could explain in the future. Magic seems to occupy that area called lying (illusion, techniques to control the 'supernatural' or nature) in order to

[55] https://www.dictionary.com

[56] Now is a good time to read appendix II on miracles.

[57] Charles Dickens: *A Christmas Carol* (Chapman & Hall; London 1843) p.5

gain some control over the world around us. Another difference is that both mystery and miracle don't involve anyone's personal power, whereas magic does. Magic requires a person, or agent to perform it (think of Harry Potter and Merlin). So, you could say that humans involved with mystery and miracles are passive and humans involved with magic are active agents. Also, if you notice mystery and miracles are part of the Bible's teachings and magic is not.[58]

In my way of thinking God is not magical, nor does I AM perform magic. But I AM definitely is mystery and I AM does perform miracles. This has been my personal experience. I think one of the problems with magic is that it requires a large amount of ego to get involved with it. It seems to be a way to greater personal power, or the perception that one has greater power. In the realm of magic, we can have such things as people being changed into frogs, and other animals or natural forces doing the bidding of some sorcerer or witch that knows the right incantation or words or has a magic wand. But what about God? Does I AM perform magic? Are the wonders and miracles in the Bible a form of magic? In my way of thinking they are not. But God does use the 'natural forces.' These are not magic. If you look into miracles, you will find that they accelerate natural processes like healings.[59] Miracles also enhance natural processes like when Jesus turned water into wine.[60] God may arrange time events (synchronicity[61]), like the parting of the Red Sea and the pursuit of Pharaoh's army. I don't think one should get miracles confused with magic for these reasons.

---

[58] Magic is referred to in the Bible as something to be avoided (see Acts 8 NIV) and the term 'magician' is used only in the Old Testament. However, sorcerer(s) is used in both Old and New Testaments.

[59] As you know the body will heal itself, 'healings' seem to accelerate what the body already does.

[60] See John 2:1-11 NIV

[61] Coincidences in time; events occurring at the same time.

Mystery is what we deal with on a regular basis. What do you know about your own consciousness? How do you determine what is your brain and what is your mind? What is this thing called 'soul?' Do you really have one or not? How does your DNA 'know' how to repair itself? How does a muscle cell know how to make only muscle cells and not brain cells? Get the idea?

How we think about these three terms is important in beginning to understand our thinking patterns and reducing the assumptions that we make in thinking each day.

Often, recently, I have been side tracked with mystery and its relationship to 'hiddenness.' I have mused over how the most powerful forces in the universe are hidden[62]. How the great mysteries of life are hidden. How God is hidden. How Jesus was hidden from the world for all intents and purposes in a small, seemingly insignificant country in the Middle East (at least according to written history). And, of course, after thinking these thoughts, was the question; Why? What is it about God and I AM's way of dealing with the universe so hidden and why did it take so long to reveal and/or comprehend? What on earth is going on? This idea is so contrary to the ways of the world and particularly humans. We want everything NOW! Our sense of our short lifespan causes us to want things done NOW.

Another way to look at this 'hiddenness' is that God is patient. He has eternal patience. Again, the word of a 3-year-old strikes me: Why? And as usual, the final 'why' goes unanswered. And, again another way to look at this is: we are finite and God is infinite. Now the tendency here is to look at the word infinite as just another quantity, with no real understanding of the term... We just don't get 'infinite.' We only have a shallow view of what 'infinite' means. Just like our shallow view of God.

---

[62] Strong and weak nuclear force, electromagnetic and the weaker force of gravity.

And again, I am back to the beginning of my questions, with no real answers that I can be certain.

This idea of 'hiddenness' shows up over and over in the stories the Bible tells about Jesus and God. It all depends on how you look at it; your perspective. Many times, the hiddenness of God is used with the word 'but.' The word 'but' is used 3751 times in the Bible. Only 45 of those times do we read the phrase 'but God.' In most of these usages, God comes through with a 'hidden' agenda, or his intervention was hidden from the people in the Bible story. For example, in the book of Genesis[63] there is the famous story of Joseph (his Technicolor coat), when he is recognized by his many brothers and they fear him, since he is a powerful person in Egypt and his brothers had sold him earlier to an Egyptian to be a slave. Joseph says to them: "as for you, you meant evil against me, but God meant it for good."[64] There are many other examples you could look up just Goggle the phrase 'but God.'

Sometimes the hiddenness is not explicit, but implicit. For example, in the book of John, Jesus gets the Pharisees all riled up and angry. They pick up stones to kill him, BUT: "Jesus hid himself, slipping away from the temple grounds."[65] Just 'how' Jesus did this I am not sure we need to know. But it does show me how God can hide right in our midst. Which is pretty much true for most of the time. God in his presence in the universe is hidden to most of the world. So, this hiddenness looks to me like a normal thing for God to do.

The most translated book in the world is the Bible. Most of the people who did this prodigious job of translation are unknown; hidden from the world view. When you realize that there are over 1200 translations of the Bible just into English, then you begin to realize how many people were involved; literally thousands!

---

[63] For the complete story read Ge 37-45 NIV; nine chapters! That's almost 1/5 if the book.

[64] Ge 50:20a NIV

[65] Jn 8:59b NIV

Name five. Bet you can't. Neither can I. They are hidden. They did their job without fame and fortune. And I would add, probably the greatest people in the world you will not hear about. They go about doing their service to humanity without fame and fortune. But God knows their names and their deeds. After all it is God's memory that counts in the long run and not ours. "However, do not rejoice that the spirits submit to you, but rejoice that your names are written in heaven."[66]

Hidden is a word used in the New Testament that is related to mystery[67]. A mystery is an idea which has been hidden in the universe, until it is revealed at some point in time. One of the most significant mysteries is the singularity we Followers of Jesus call the 'Christ Event.' This is the short period of time when Jesus the Christ was on earth. His birth, death, and resurrection. St. Paul talks about the mystery of Christ, which was hidden for all time[68], until the 'fullness of time' according to the scriptures.[69] This mystery is "Christ in you."[70]

Another area in thinking where mystery, magic and miracle get all mixed up is the difference between myth and story. Myths involve an imaginary world here people can envision gods and goddesses[71]living in some realm (as Mt. Olympus) and engaged in battles and sex and competitions. There is no mystery. Nothing is hidden. As a worshipper of theses gods and goddesses, you know their names, but most likely they don't know yours. This context is true for the Norse gods, the Roman gods, the Greek gods, and the gods of Canaan where the Israelites went after the Exodus. In contrast, stories in the Bible are about the everyday happenings of people living their everyday lives. There is certainly no magic

---

66 Lk 10:20 NIV

67 The word mystery appears only in the New Testament of the Bible.

68 Ro 16:25 NIV

69 1 Co 15:3b, 4b; NIV

70 Col 1:27. NIV

71 Did you know there is no Hebrew word for goddess?

involved. The One God enters these lives of ordinary people, gets involved with their ordinary lives, and knows their ordinary names. But, to me, the ordinary becomes the ground for the hiddenness of God, where the "supernatural is camouflaged in the natural."[72] Magic is usually involved in myth. Magic is performed to get the gods and goddesses to do what you want them to do. To be at your 'beck and call.'[73] Not so with Bible stories. They are mostly people doing the hard thing of their faith: worshipping and waiting on the One True God. No magic; just faith.

The 'Modern Mind'

In my way of thinking this is one of our biggest problems in thinking; wanting to put our 'mindset' on the way the people of ancient history thought. Let's get it straight from the start: We have only a vague idea of how and what they thought. We only have the words that they have left as clues. We don't know what their emotions were as they wrote their words, nor do we know the precise frame of reference from which they write. Sometimes we don't even know the genre that they are writing, so we place their texts into a genre that we 'think' is correct.

This brings me to Biblical interpretation. When we use an authoritative source that is given so much weight as the Bible, we get into more trouble when we assume the 'modern mind' on the writers of the Bible, both Old and New Testaments. We forget all the lack of awareness of things in our world that the writers of the Bible did not know. Let me list a few and I am sure you will get the idea.

---

[72] E. Peterson, *Eat This Book,* (Eerdmans Publishing Co. 2006) p.160

[73] 14th century phrase; probably originally 'beckon and call,' which fits well in my context. Similar in thinking to people who think that God should be their personal 'gofer.'

- Science- there was no science as we know it.
- Microscopes, telescopes, centrifuges, etc. -didn't exist.
- Our view of the cosmos. They didn't know about galaxies, black holes, stars, orbits, comets, etc. They thought the universe was the stars, planets, sun and earth. They had no idea of the vastness of space or the huge age of the universe.
- DNA, genetics, etc. – didn't know about. They had never had an understanding of atoms, molecules etc.
- Air travel, cars, etc.
- TV, Computers, etc. – no idea.
- -isms: existentialism, conservatism, etc. There were very few -isms. Philosophy was in its infancy.
- Rushed, busy lives: not a problem.
- Books, CDs, and the like; Books were scrolls, and they were few and far between, and the ones that existed were protected and located in synagogues and 'libraries.'

We all have varying degrees of understanding of the list I have above, but the writers of the Bible DID NOT. So, when we put our understandings of the world around us as we read the Bible we put ourselves in serious mis-understandings of the texts we read. I have found this idea to be true for me as I began reading the Bible seriously, 50 years ago. Today I am more convinced than ever that this 'modern mindset' is one of our biggest challenges when reading the Bible and making sense out of it. I want to say that this idea fits into our A/NT, but I am not sure it does. It's more of a serious mistake in assumptions that we make when we begin reading an authoritative text. I found that I needed to read authors who have literally spent their lives in trying to understand the 'mindset' of the writers of the Bible, in order to get a good idea of what these writers meant from the frame of reference of their time. This is a lot of hard work mentally. I will include some of my research and new understandings in the sections to follow.

Punctuation is another factor that determines the 'modern

mind.' Punctuation was not used extensively in texts until the invention of the printing press. It was used by the 'ancients' to show points of departure in the texts and where subjects (chapters) began and ended. Much early punctuation was used to guide actors on the Greek stage. The modern use of punctuation began between 1450 and 1500 AD when the printing press and type setting were prevalent. Punctuation use today can serve as a guide to our reading and speaking or in some cases interfere with our full understanding of a text. Even the use of paragraphs that we take for granted is a relatively new concept in reading/writing text.[74]

One of the things us moderns like to do is take a comment out of context and use it for our own purposes, be it political or otherwise. This 'decontextualizing' of the text has led to many errors in thought. It is like seeing the trees in a forest and not seeing the whole forest. But when we stand back from the trees and see the forest a whole new level of understanding emerges. This metaphor (trees/forest) is a reality when we try to understand the letters that St. Paul wrote in the New Testament. For our convenience, the scribes and printers of the Bible have put in chapter numbers, periods and the like when they did not appear in the original text. This is why it is important to read the whole letter before you start 'dissecting' it and 'decontextualizing' it.

This modern mind has caused a lot of confusion about what ideas like crucifixion, wrath, mystery, and resurrection mean when used in the Bible. N. T Wright in his book "The Day the Revolution Began," spends a chapter on just understanding 'crucifixion.' When referring to the 3 contexts about the 'cross' of Jesus that we need to understand, he says: "All of this needs to be in our ***minds and imaginations*** if we are to glimpse, let alone understand, why that "word" (cross) was so utterly revolutionary."[75] A Biblical scholar

[74] Paragraphs were 'installed' in text around 1200 CE.

[75] N.T. Wright, *The Day the Revolution Began,* (HarperOne, 2016) p.59.

like Wright understands the effect that putting our modern mind on Biblical context can cause some serious thinking problems.

And then there is our modern understanding of memory. We don't use our memories very much and most people avoid the work of committing a lot of information to memory. You hear such statements as: "Why do I need to remember this, when I can just Goggle it." "Memorizing is just too hard, or too much work." Or the one I heard a lot from my students (which may be true): "Why do I have to remember this stuff, I will never need it?" (This one contains the ubiquitous A/NT.) I think you get the idea. But, our memory is a vast resource within out brain/mind that has many rewards if you take the time to learn to use it. Scholars and teachers in the past knew the value of having a good memory. For example, before the printing press and technology of language and written words, (Did you get that?) memory was how information was kept and passed on from generation to generation. It was called 'oral history,' but it really was the memories of peoples that was eventually written down and taken from the flow of living history (oral history). Memory training was a common practice before the 'written word.' Students who were going to be scribes and monks or rabbis, would be taught how to memorize large chunks of information, using a system for memory retrieval called mnemotechnies.[76] Students spent hours learning how to categorize and store huge volumes of information, so that they could retrieve it in a short period of time. Sometimes the teacher of memory would use the metaphor of a castle, or an ark in which to store memories. But the commonality was that the information memorized would be almost instantly retrievable.

I have found comfort and life-long satisfaction from the information that I have 'stored' in my memory. The Psalms, and the little mnemonic word plays and puns that have stayed with me over the years are still a source of contentment as I age. The modern

[76] The process(es) of developing memory.

mind is losing its grip on autonomy as it 'stores' it's information on digital devices for 'safe keeping.' Are we becoming more and more dependent on machines to do our memorizing for us? And what if these machines become the caretakers of our memories?

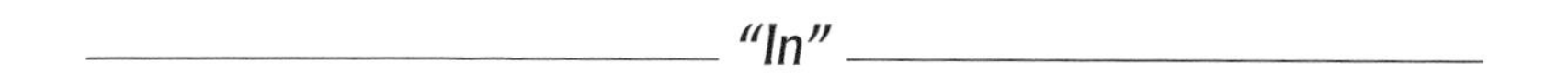

"In"

The word 'in' is a very small word, not quite as small as 'a' or 'I', but in the same category of small words. However, I learned long ago that small words can have a great impact on the meaning of the sentence that I am reading and making sense out of it for myself. Other small words that impact on the meaning of a sentence are; but, may, and, or, and of. And further, when they come in pairs like and/or be sure you decipher their exact meaning before you go on in your thinking, or (I used one!) you can be led down a thinking path other than the one the author of the sentence wanted you to use.

Now, back to the word 'in.' This, I think, is a very significant word in the Bible. The word 'in' can mean about 9 different ways as a preposition. And that's the reason you need to stop and think about the 'context' in the sentence 'it' is used 'in.' Get it? This word is often overlooked and passed over lightly as we read the Bible. In fact, the very first word used in most modern English Bibles is: "In the beginning." As Maria says in The Sound of Music: "Let's start at the very beginning."[77] Let's look at some other places in the Bible where the word 'in' is used and often overlooked. (I'll just use two to get the idea across.) Look at Colossians 1:16-18 (NIV). Here the word 'in' is used 4 times. Twice these verses use the term; 'in him' and the other two times: 'in heaven;' and 'in everything.' Note that the other two terms are all inclusive of heaven and earth. Now the terms used here are absolute terms (A/NT). Think about what this

[77] From the song "Do-Re-Mi" in "The Sound of Music," a film made in 1965 by Twentieth Century Fox.

means. The whole material universe, both physical and spiritual. Now add the other 'in' usages and you get a great big WOW about who this person, "The Son" is. This Person that St. Paul is talking about is cosmic in nature and is the focal point of all creation/ evolution. He must be a 'little' more important than kings, rulers, presidents, and congress.

The second use of the word 'in' in bible messaging occurs in 2 Corinthians 5:19 (NIV) and Galatians 3:28 (NIV). There are many other verses where St. Paul uses the word 'in' to illustrate my point, but I will just focus on these two. In these two verses Paul is using the preposition 'in' to talk about people being 'included' 'in' something. In both these verses the 'in' is used with 'Christ.' In one verse God is reconciling the world 'in Christ' and in the other, Jew and Gentile, slave and free, and male and female are **all** INCLUDED 'in Christ.' It seems clear that the world and virtually 'all' people are included in the reconciling action of God through the Christ. This theme of inclusion runs through both the old and new testaments. This relational oneness of the purposes of God are in harmony with the relational oneness that science has observed in the universe.[78]

Now let's move a little deeper into the word 'in.' A another way to use 'in' is that you can find 'something inside' of something. For example: "You will find my wallet 'in' my pants pocket." (please don't do that when I'm wearing my pants.) I think the meaning clear. Like Ragu spaghetti sauce: "It's in the sauce." What we mean when 'in' is used this way is that something is 'hidden in' something, like my pants or the sauce. And this is the imagery we need to understand when we read the parable of Jesus called the parable of the sower; (Matthew 13:1-23 NIV, also in Luke and Mark). "What?" You say: "The word 'in' is not used in this parable." And you are right. In this parable the word 'in' is hidden. Ask yourself the question: "What is the seed and what is hidden 'in'

[78] See experiments on 'EPR paradox.' (quantum nonlocality).

the seed?" Jesus interprets the parable to his disciples (they didn't get it) and says that the seed is the Word/message/information about the kingdom of God. So, the 'message' is hidden 'in' the world (soil). What strikes me is what we have learned about seeds. Hidden 'in' seeds are all the DNA that is required to make a new plant that those particular seeds came from. This DNA is hidden 'in' the seed and only recently have we learned about this DNA. So, all the information is 'in' the seed. The other strange thing about seeds is that they seem to disappear 'in' the soil. As Jesus says in John 12:24, the seed must die to produce many seeds (in the fruit). Now who was it that died for us?

Most of the operations of God are hidden. They don't make the news, they are usually only noticed 'after the fact' and sometimes they go completely unnoticed. The so-called 'eyes of faith' looks for these seeds of the Word of God. These 'eyes of faith' have the lenses needed to 'see' the Word of God 'in' the field/soil/world. Are these the 'eyes of faith' also the ones needed to see the 'narrow gate;' 'the road less traveled;' the path that makes all the difference in life? All because we can develop our ability to see 'in?' Just something to think about.

Word Problems

When I taught science, I used a lot of word problems to teach my students ideas. They loathed them. They would say; "Mr. P can we have multiple choice or true and false or matching problems. We hate word problems." I remember when I took mathematics and the teacher gave us 'word problems' I knew I was in for making mistakes, I just wanted problems with equations and formulas. Those were easier for me. What is going on here? Why do so many of us like to avoid 'word problems?' Well, words are very ambiguous in their use, and in English they can have more than one meaning. I remember when I was prepping students for their

AP exams[79] the first **three rules** I told them for passing their exams were "follow the directions." A lot of students would not follow the directions (because they didn't know what the directions meant), and therefore answer the question(s) incorrectly.

One of the first times I began to see the damage to thought that words can do[80] is when I was reading "Paths from Science to God" by Arthur Peacocke. ". words strain, crack, and sometimes break, under the burden of striving to express and refer to such a Transcendent.[81]" (the Transcendent he was referring to was Ultimate Reality [God]). I think that here is a good summation of what words can fail to do when we are trying to describe something extremely complex in it's being. God is really beyond any words we can muster in our thought. The Bible many times reminds us of this. "My thoughts are not your thoughts, and my ways are not your ways.[82]" Pretty much the whole Psalm 139 tells us we can't understand God.

I have read many books on spirituality of some sort and found that most of the time the authors of these books are arguing the 'incorrect' use of terms (words) when others describe spiritual things they don't agree with, or the interpretation of a particular scripture is not correct or misleading. But the real problem is in our use of words and how they have different meanings and contexts for different thinkers. When you are attempting to describe the Other (spiritual things), words to not work to well.

There is also the problem of traditional and original 'revelation' that John Locke[83] so eloquently pointed out in 1690. His basic idea was that when someone has an *original revelation* [experience] (Moses and the burning bush in Exodus, or Paul on the road to

---

[79] High school advanced placement (AP) tests and curriculum

[80] Sorry English teachers and writers, but you need to know this.

[81] A. Peacocke, *Paths From Science Towards God,* (Oneworld, 2002) p.40.

[82] Isaiah 55:8 NIV

[83] Locke (1632-1704) was an influential philosopher of the 'enlightenment' period he greatly influenced the 'Founding Fathers' of America.

Damascus in Acts) and then that experience is put into words and written down in an authoritative text. Then each of us reads the text and comes away with a slightly different (and sometimes quite different) interpretation of the story of that original experience. And when you have whole communities of people agreeing on 'spiritual' experiences they usually form a sect or religion, that adheres to the teachings of a particular leader. This belief system and its interpretation(s) Locke called *traditional revelation.* For example, Judaism is based on the spiritual experiences of the Hebrew patriarchs (Abraham, Moses, etc.). So, over the thousands of years since these spiritual experiences occurred there as developed a religion we call Judaism. The same thing is true for other religions. This is why we need to depend on our ability to decide for ourselves what our best IBE (Inference to the Best Explanation)[84] for the events and/or experiences being described. We need to keep a constant awareness of knowing that words can cloud our understanding of the world around us. That does not mean that we abandon the use of words. Words are helpful in keeping track of information and analyzing the world. But we need to be aware that they are just a tool in our thinking and not the answer to how to think.

Another example of how words get in the way of clear thinking are words like 'justice.' We use this word in contrived ways such as 'justice league' (Marvel Comics) or 'justice for all' (another A/NT usage). But, think about it. What is 'justice'? If you look in a dictionary (which I recommend) you will find several meanings depending on (you guessed it) the context. But all the definitions have something to do with being morally right, or rightness. Also, the term implies the image of what happens in a courtroom, where 'justice' gets a chance to be done. To make things even worse the

---

[84] IBE – also abductive reasoning, which starts with an observation then seeks to find the 'simplest' and most likely explanation. In a way it is based on Occam's Razor. (you might want to look that up.)

New Testament uses the term 'justification,' which relates to the 'law.' In the verse from Romans, St. Paul says: "Consequently, just as one trespass resulted in condemnation for all people, so also, one righteous act resulted in justification and life for all people.[85]" Here Paul is referring to the initial sin: eating the fruit in the Garden of Eden and the righteous act of Jesus; crucifixion and resurrection. Paul is arguing that God is not exacting 'justice' but putting things 'right.' 'Justice' has a lot to do with the goal of restoring relationships between two persons or entities. In our verse above, the relationship between God and humans was restored by the Christ Event. God is setting things 'right.' If we understand 'justice' in this way it clears up a lot of confusion when we read other parts of the Scriptures. For example; when the prophet Isaiah says: "the crooked made straight,"[86] or John the Baptist saying: "preparing the way,"[87]you can see them to mean 'setting things right.' These are phrases involving 'justice.'

So, what's the big deal? Again, we see how we understand the meaning of a word can influence how we can understand the meaning of a Biblical text, or for that matter any authoritative text. A lot of the time we want to put our modern mind set on the Scriptures when that was not how the writers of the Scriptures meant for us to interpret the word they were using. And further, our emotional response to the word can interfere with us understanding the text. The emotional content for the word 'justice' is the expectation that the 'bad' guy will get what he/she deserves. Kind of a rush of retribution happiness, or victorious euphoria. But 'setting things right'? No so much. And that may be why we like the modern usage of the term 'justice.' In our culture of retributive justice that is how 'justice' is done. Revenge. So, when we read the part in the Sermon on the Mount where Jesus tells us

85 Ro 5:18 NIV.

86 Isa 40:4. NIV

87 Mt 3:3. NIV

to love our enemies, and bless and pray for them, we think how impractical that is. That is not how we get 'justice,' but that is how we 'set things right.' What we fail to grasp is that God has already 'set things straight' through the Christ Event. God will continue to make the 'crooked straight.' You can't stop Him. That is why people like Dr. Martin Luther King[88] knew that the universe was continuously moving toward justice. Dr. King could 'see' that God was going to 'set things straight.'

There is another unfortunate process that happens when we have a limited vocabulary of words. In the English language we have what I call 'catch all' words, that do a limited job conveying the meaning intended by the speaker or writer. For example, words like 'see' and 'hear' and 'love' and 'good' and 'evil' and 'think' and 'sex' and the like can get very confused and misunderstood when there is not a good definition between people as to what these words mean. Just take the word 'see.' Look it up. There are 28 ways to use this word and that does not include phrases like 'see about,' or 'see after,' or 'see out,' etc. We use it as a verb, but it can also be used as a noun. And then there are the various spellings with the same pronunciations like sea and see. Words can be a problem. Other languages use different words for ideas like 'see.' For example, in Greek the word 'see' has at least 3 different words[89] and then they add suffixes and prefixes that can change the meaning of the base words, depending on usage. And this is why people who come to America from other countries have problems with learning the meanings of many of our 'catch all' words. And this is also why punning is so prevalent in the English language. 'The blind carpenter picked up his hammer and saw.' Get it?

E. Peterson says that: "Each language is an intricate and living culture, a culture distilled into words, spread out in language. If

---

[88] An American Baptist minister and activist; Famous for his "I have a dream" speech and many of this sermons during the 1960's. Read his "Where Do We Go From Here" speech on 8/16/1967 to get the idea of setting things straight.

[89] Horao, theaomai, and blepo, for example.

all we are translating is dictionary meanings, the entire culture is lost in translation."[90] And isn't this just what we do when we travel abroad with a 'translator' of some sort, be it a guide, or a language dictionary or an app? I have seen 'tourists' spend so much time translating, that they miss the culture surrounding them on their trips to a foreign land. The culture around us, when we travel abroad, is non-verbal[91] with voice tone and smells and textures. This foreign culture is communicating more with being than with words. Just as we communicate more from who we are, rather than what we say. This is why you hear people saying; "What you are speaks so loudly, I can't hear what you are saying." Words can be a real problem for clear thinking.

If you listen carefully to ads and other means of advertisements and political messages, you will find the use of disclaimer words like 'may' and 'but.' These words are indicators of a disclaimer. I hope you've noticed that these are small words just like 'in.' Just what is a disclaimer? Well, back to the old dictionary. A disclaimer is a statement, or assertion, or document that disclaims (disavow, disown) responsibility, affiliation, etc. I just love it when the dictionary uses the same term to describe a term. I think you get my intent. The word 'may' is the most used one for a disclaimer. For example; "You may have won already!" "This drug may cause death." When we read or hear these types of statements are we paying attention to the little word 'may' or are we paying attention to the word 'won,' or seeing happy people doing happy things when the narrator says: "This drug **may** cause death?" A disclaimer can

[90] E. Peterson, *Eat This Book,* (Eerdmans Publishing Co. 2006) p.169.

[91] Body language, voice tone, degrees of touching and spacing between people, and the like.

be a very little word and go un-noticed as we are subjected to advertisements and political messages.

Now the word 'but' is little but mighty in meaning (See what I mean?). In fact, it has 9 different usages, depending on your intent for the word. Here we are again, putting things in context. And the word 'but' can be used as a preposition, conjunction, noun and adverb. So, you see, context is very important. But, when it's used as a disclaimer is when it is used to cancel out what was said before. For example: A variation of a quote attributed to Winston Churchill: 'Indeed, it has been said that democracy is the worst form of government, **but** for all the other ones that have been tried from time to time.[92]'

[92] This is not what Churchill said, but a paraphrase of his famous quote about democracy. The original author of this quote is subject to debate.

CHAPTER II

ALL OR NOTHING THINKING

A/NT Examples

The more I look at this thinking pattern in our lives, the more I see it sneaking into our thinking. If you Google any A/NT term in the following manner, you will be amazed at what you get. Try searching; All my heroes... or I never get... or I always.... Or All men are... or All women are. Well, you get the idea. Try it. It proves my point of how common this thinking pattern is and most of the time we don't think about it being a problem; but it is.

When I was teaching school, one day I had a parent conference about a student who I had caught cheating on a test (it was obvious) of course he/she denied it. This resulted in the parent conference in which the mother said: "My child never lies to me." Now from an educator, and parent myself, this statement represented one of the most absurd statements that I have heard when I was teaching. Kids do lie. They don't lie all the time and they don't tell the truth all the time. I knew my children lied to me and I knew from many years in the classroom that my students lied to me. Lying is usually the first thing people do when they are 'caught' doing something that they know is wrong. Yes, even our presidents lie! To think your child never lies to you, is to live in a fantasy land. And I have been surprised by how many parents believe this. There is story after story on TV and movies where children are 'caught' in their lies, when their parents thought they only told the truth.

And here is another example of A/NT thinking destroying lives. Not long ago the actor who portrayed Princess Leia Organa in 'Star Wars,'[1] Carrie Fisher, died of a heart condition. Some of the pundits in the media surmised that her death was attributed to cocaine use. In an interview she had given years before her death she said she decided to take drugs because: "I didn't like cocaine, but I wanted to feel any way other than the way I did, so I'd do *anything*.[2]" And there it is that A/NT thinking. It's drugs or nothing.

More recently, Charles Barkley, a retired professional basketball player and analyst in the media, when interviewed by USA Today Sports on March 31, 2018, when referring to the FBI investigating cheating in professional basketball, said: "Listen, I went to college in 1981. We cheated back then. We're cheating now. They're **always** cheating. The toothpaste is out of the tube.[3]" Woah! Here is an A/NT with some embedded philosophy. Here we have the use of A/NT thinking with a metaphor: 'The toothpaste is out of the tube.' This means that something happened in the past and it can't be changed (just try putting toothpaste back in the tube). It can also mean that something is happening and can't be changed. I think that was what Mr. Barkley was referring to here. He might as well have said, 'there is always going to be cheating.' Well, in my way of thinking that is fatalistic. Oh well, we just have to accept the way things are and live with it. Does that mean that we should not hope for better than 'always' cheating for professional sports? Should be just let cheating run rampant in sports because it is 'always' going to be there? A/NT can really take us down some erroneous paths of thought.

---

[1] I think we know who that is; if not look up Star Wars on the internet.

[2] Elizabeth Johnson, "Herald Tribune," 4/20/2013 interview.

[3] https://www.ajc.com/sports/college/charles-barkley-bashes-fbi-college-basketball-investigation

A more implicit form of A/NT can be found in pretty intellectual books. For example in his book "How to Create Mind," Ray Kurzwell introduces the concept of LOAR (Law of Accelerating Returns), and 'Pattern Recognition Theory of Mind' (PRTM)[4], as the two major components of thought occurring in the neocortex.[5] Kurzwell does a brilliant job of getting the reader to this point in his thinking and nicely summarizes the evolution of emergent properties in the universe from the Anthropic Principles[6] to the emergence of intelligence in humans. Then he neatly slides into the if/then statement: "**If** understanding language and other phenomena through statistical analysis does not count as true understanding, **then** humans have no understanding either."[7] What? We have no understanding but his two invented principles? Does that mean that all thinking is gained by statistical analysis? To me, he might as well say: 'If you can't measure it, it doesn't exist.' I had hoped for more as I read his book. My other ways of thinking; meditation, metaphors, stories, communion with God, and reflection are just 'statistical analysis?' This was certainly not my whole brain/mind experience of life. I have stories and metaphors running around in my head that give me meaning and purpose in my life. I have gleaned from these stories and metaphors 'understandings' that I have a lot of trouble putting into words. Kurzwell's statement, to me, is an intellectual form of A/NT thinking. I hope you didn't get lost in the terminology. It was necessary, in order to get my point across.

My last example of A/NT thinking comes from the Declaration of Independence. What? There is A/NT thinking in that too? I think so. I think most of us know the phrase: "All men are

---

[4] Ray Kurzwell, *How to Create Mind,* (Viking Penquin, 2012) p. 26 and 30.

[5] Neocortex – the largest and most evolutionary recent portion of the cerebrum (largest part of our brain.)

[6] Anthropic Principle: that the laws of nature and parameters of the universe take on values that are consistent with conditions for life as we know it.

[7] Ray Kurzwell, *How to Create Mind,* (Viking Penquin, 2012) pp. 32-33.

created equal," from the Declaration. We have been teaching this statement in America, since soon after 1776, when it was written. This phrase was probably suggested to Thomas Jefferson by an Italian immigrant named Mazzei. But, when you think about this phrase, it is an A/NT phase, that pushes our thinking to a greater limit. Groups and organizations in this country have questioned the absolutism that this phrase suggests. And some groups have even put this phrase in reverse by saying that they don't want to be everyone else's equal! Even the term 'men' in the phrase has connotations that some people see as a problem. However, if you understand the mind-set of 1776, Jefferson's intent with the word 'men' was from its original meaning: a thinking person, and not a gender designation. But, as usual I could be wrong, since I don't know what was going on in Jefferson's mind at the time he wrote the phrase. Boy, can language get confusing or what? Let's infer that Jefferson meant; 'all humans are created equal.' Now we have a better way forward and considering what has happened to 'rights[8]' in America since 1776, we would see that that was probably his intent.

The framers of the Declaration of Independence qualified the 'all men are created equal' statement with the term 'self-evident.'[9] Self-evident means; something we know is true without any proof. It is considered a universal understanding. But is it? If this is a universal truth, then how come some people don't believe it? How come some groups[10] think other people are not equal to them, or have less rights than them, or want to deny other people their 'self-evident' rights in some form or another? Then for some people what the framers of the Declaration of Independence thought was 'self-evident,' is not. Language really gets in the way.

If we look down the long road of American History we see a

---

[8] Voting rights, civil rights, etc.

[9] "We hold these truths to be self-evident, that all men are created equal."

[10] Such groups as Nazis, Fascists, and a lot of 'isms.'

movement toward a better definition of 'all men are created equal.' And there is still a lot of history to go, before we truly realize the 'self-evident' fact that 'all men are created equal.' The battles for the truth that 'all men are created equal' will go on. And the day will finally come when we can truly say that this truth, 'all men are created equal' will BE self-evident.

The outcome of this striving for equality for all men and women was what Jesus was saying when He said: "The Kingdom of God is at hand."[11] In God's Kingdom there is no distinctions between groups of peoples. We will be one family. That is God's will for us and you don't get in the way of God for the 'powers' of hell cannot prevail against it.

One final thought about A/NT thinking. This, in my mind, is the source of terrorism, be it 'home grown,' or foreign. I believe that terrorism begins in the mind. It begins when someone concludes (erroneously) that a certain type of human is not human, but sub-human, or things. These sub-humans (ethnic group, political faction, type of worker like police, teacher, doctor, etc.) then lose the face of humanity for the terrorist. And then the A/NT thinking that ALL these people in the sub-human group are alike. And that is the fallacy; the falsehood. And this process of thinking that promotes terrorism is not unique to any culture or ethnic group, or political faction. And that is my reason why we have 'home grown' and foreign terrorists in our midst.

So, let the dinosaurs of our day scream and yell and criticize and belittle and use violence to have their way. To be sure, their day is coming to an end. They are dying a slow death. They may kill many who stand in their way, but they are not the final say. When they have become exhausted and decaying in their small ways of thinking, there will be a day when not one of them is left to carry out their violent ways to preserve their 'freedoms.' And then the words written by Isaiah will BE true: "He will judge between

[11] Mt; 3:2; 4:17, Mk 1:15 NIV

nations and will settle disputes for many peoples. They will beat their swords into plowshares and their spears into pruning hooks. Nation will not take up sword against nation, nor will they train for war anymore."[12]

Some of us have an internal dialogue going on in our brains every waking second, and sometimes in our dreams. I almost wrote 'all of us' and then caught myself in order not to make my statement an A/NT. I can't speak for 'everyone', since I have only asked 'some' people about what is going on in their minds. Whew! Thinking is hard. It is difficult to have a "tethered mind, freed from the lies."[13]This means to me that I must continually do the hard job of thinking through the events of my life, grounding (tethered) my life with whole brain thinking. Not giving into the easy thoughts of A/NT.

The Only All

There is really only one time we can legitimately use the A/NT word 'all,' in my opinion, and that is in reference to God. I AM is ONE and therefore ALL. I believe that God is both immanent and transcendent. Whoa! What does that mean? For me, immanent means that God is everywhere in the universe, you can't get away from God. Psalm 139 points this out in verses 1-12. Read them as often as you like and you will get the message that God is immanent. Then there is transcendent. This means to me that God is also 'above' and 'beyond' the universe. God is greater than the boundaries of the universe to me. We humans can't comprehend that. But in my way of thinking we don't need to. We just need to 'stand in awe...' And worship the mystery of God.

And then there is Job and his plight as explained in the book of Job. After reading the book and studying it, I boiled it down to the

[12] Isa 2:4. NIV

[13] A line from the song "I Will Wait;" by Mumford and Sons; 2009.

following account (paraphrased to the skinny version). Job has a lot of terrible things happen to him, of which God is aware. Job refuses to curse God and die. Three of his friends come and try to help him (philosophically) with his 'problems.' Then a fourth friend (an angry young man) comes and gives his philosophy for the next 6 chapters of the book. Job replies to his first three friends but does not to the angry young man. To me the important point is that the angry young man defends God. And then, surprise, surprise, God answers Job, but it has nothing to do with his 'problems.' God says to Job: "Where were you?[14]" This is the question that deserves a lot of attention, but many people seem to overlook the impact of that phrase in relation to God being the Only All.

We were not there when the universe began. We really don't know how it began. We can only surmise how it began. Science can extrapolate[15] the data back through billions of years but can't extrapolate to the very beginning of the Big Bang[16]. Some scientists would like to believe that we have this all figured out, but we don't. A lot of their thinking is based on the assumption that the laws governing the universe have not changed since the beginning. BUT, they were not there so they really don't know for sure. Only God was there. Isn't it funny that a little question from a book of the Bible can show how much we don't know, as we swell with pride at how much we have learned from the scientific method?

---

[14] Job 38: 4a NIV

[15] An inference using data to extend a principle outside of the known data. An estimate.

[16] The prevailing theory on how the universe began. See https://en.wikipedia.org/wikw/Big_Bang

God and Time

There seems to be a big problem in the Christian Church's understanding of time and its relationship to God. I don't think I have 'the' answers to this dilemma, but I think I can offer some insights into our understanding of the relationship between God and time, based on my readings from various authors on the subject of time.[17] And I don't mean our understanding of how to measure time. We all are very good at measuring time. I remember that my students used to measure time very accurately when it came to knowing when class would end!

What I am talking about here is what time is. This is a more 'philosophical' idea about time then you might want to know about. For example: Do we move through time or does time move past us? Is time a physical thing or is it an energy thing? It appears we really don't know exactly what it is, only we all experience it. Like gravity, we have not experienced what it is like not to have it around. Astronauts still experience gravity when they are 'weightless' in space, but the effects are minimal because of how fast they are moving and the gravity of other objects around them is very small.

First of all, the Christian church sees time in two forms: God's time and our time, so you will hear such comments as:" A thousand years in your sight are like a day that has just gone by, or like a watch in the night.[18]" Here the psalmist shows the difference in how God measures time and we measure time. But this often-quoted verse from the Bible does bring up an important idea about God and time. That is, that God is the only being that has been present throughout all time and will be present in all time to come. Think about what this means. God knows everything that has happened in the universe! That is quite a memory. We can't even begin to understand what that means. It is just too much for us to

[17] Authors: Arthur Peacocke and John Polkinghorne.

[18] Ps 90:4 NIV

understand. This idea about God and time also means that God has a very good grasp on the probabilities of events in the universe, knowing all the patterns of events that exist! Wow, put that on for size. Again, we are just too limited in our understanding of the universe to grasp just what this means. Our God, in order to just begin to understand I AM, is too small!

One way to understand time is to say that time is a relationship between events and is created BY events. So, as I like to say, "time is nature's way of making sure everything doesn't happen at once." In this definition, time is a relationship. Or as we might say; "In the beginning, and then this happened." In fact, that is where the Bible begins; "In the beginning:" a time relationship. So, then, it makes sense that "in the beginning" the only being present was God. Therefore, when the book of Genesis opens we are in the realm of God's time, where "a thousand years are like a day." So what amount of time that goes by in each day[19] of the first chapter of Genesis is from God's perspective, not ours. And in addition, since God doesn't create the day and night until the fourth day of creation, there is no time measurement (day/night) as we measure a day, until the fourth 'day.' So, this word 'day' as used in the book of Genesis is up for grabs as to how it is measured in time.

Since God is omniscient[20], God knows all that is possible to know at any moment in time. But does God know the future? Many Christians think that God does. This is not too logical from my viewpoint. If God is creating time and space, then how could God know the content of that time before it is created? Further, there would be no free-will, since God already knows what we and the universe is going to do. So, in relation to time, God seems to be bipolar. By that I mean God is outside of time and within time at the

---

[19] The word 'day' in the Bible (both old and new testament) has various meaning depending on the context of usage. It can mean literally a 24-hour time period, or figuratively as in the 'day of the Lord,' or an unspecified amount of time (yom in Hebrew). Hemera (day in Greek) was a goddess.

[20] Knows all that is possible to know.

same time. Boy is that confusing. In other words, God transcends time and is involved in time by guiding and directing the universe to God's purposes. These purposes of God we call his 'steadfastness' or his enduring faithfulness. God steadfast love for the universe and love for us as his creation. "God so LOVED the world.[21]"

If you have been following my reasoning so far, God creates time continuously and doesn't know what we will do at any one point in time, but God knows 'all' the possible outcomes for any of our decisions, be they within his plan for us or not. A lot of Christians don't like this idea, because they think it diminishes God. But then there is another idea about God called 'kenosis.' This term basically means that God has limited I AM- out of love for us. This idea is demonstrated by the hiddenness of God and the coming of Christ, who was humble, rejected and crucified in an 'occupied' little country at the edge of the Roman Empire (at the time). God is humbled in the person of Christ Jesus and freely subjects YHWH[22] (since Christians believe that Christ is God) to death and humiliation. God remains hidden in the universe, like the author of a play is hidden from the audience.

And then there is the problem of the 'times' in the Bible where God's prophets and sages do a lot of things that show they have free-will in time and God has to correct the situation or patiently wait until people of Israel 'get the point' that God is trying to make with them, using timed events and serendipitous situations to show Israel God's purposes. All this trial and error by the people in the Bible certainly suggests to be that there is free will. Some Christian sects don't like this idea of 'free will' and get very upset when it is mentioned. But, many of the Biblical stories of prophets and kings and people in Israel certainly demonstrate the 'free will' of His chosen people, Israel.

---

[21] Jn 3:16 a NIV

[22] The tetragrammaton. The four letters in Latin for the unspeakable name of God. It has been popular in many Christian communities to pronounce this as "Yahweh." The Hebrews knew and I agree that God is indescribable.

Then there is another term that we use to describe time. The word 'now.' The problem is how do you measure 'now?' Quick answer: you can't. We use this term to show immediacy. For example: "Come here now!" This means 'right away' or ASAP, depending on the politeness of the usage. Sir Isaac Newton tried to solve the problem of measuring 'now' with his invention of calculus and chopping up time into tiny segments, so it could be measured more precisely, but in spite of all science's efforts time still remains a flowing thing, down to a nanosecond, but really never reaching the elusive 'now.' Time is really hard to 'pin down,' so we can study it.

To summarize; God created this thing we call time and it flows from the beginning (Big Bang) to 'now!' Since in time God cannot logically know what will happen next (since it has no content), we have free will, but God does know every possible outcome of our decisions we make in freedom.

Then there is the problem of 'my schedule' and 'God's schedule.' We are like Veruca in "Willy Wonka and the Chocolate Factory,"[23] who says: "Daddy, I want it NOW!" We want our Daddy (God) to do what we want now! So, we get very impatient with God's schedule. But we need to put God's time in perspective, as with most things in life. Take a look at Genesis 15 where God forms a covenant with Abraham. You need to read the whole chapter to get the context of what this covenant is, but the part that interests me in relation to 'my time' and 'God's time' is verses thirteen through fifteen[24]. My paraphrase of these verses is: 'Abraham, your descendants will be slaves in a place they do not know for 400 years, but I will punish this nation and your descendants will come out of that nation with great possessions (read the book of Exodus for the details). But as for you (Abraham) you will live to a

[23] "Willy Wonka and The Chocolate Factory," Paramount Pictures, 1971. Veruca is a demanding, greedy child who is completely spoiled.

[24] Ge 15: 13-15 NIV

ripe old age.' God is giving Abraham his life schedule and how he fits in with 'God's schedule. As modern-day followers of Jesus this is the perspective we need to take when we think we can 'force' God's schedule to ours.

Many groups of Christians today think they can do just that: Force God's schedule to fit their own. They think if they elect the 'right' leaders or do the 'right' things or say the 'right words' (magic) they can predict or shorten the time when Jesus will return to earth and 'set things right.' They forget that only God knows the schedule of events. Even Jesus disciples tried to 'force' him into their schedule of events, like Judas and Peter.[25] When we think we have God's timing all figured out (A/NT thinking) we can get in a lot of trouble by making too many assumptions about God's schedule and my schedule.

The problem seems to be for me, that we are so finite and God is infinite. Compared to the history of the universe or the rocks in your back yard, we have a very short 'shelf life.' We are but a moment's passing in time, compared to the billions of years of earth's history. And fear is knocking on the doors of our lives as we age and God doesn't seem to be doing anything to make our lives more secure or safe. Do we really believe that 'God has it all under control,' or do we just say that to feel better? Knowing that the purposes of God are never failing, I will choose to be like Shadrach, Meshack, and Abednego, who when faced with death in the 'fiery furnace,'[26] said: "If you throw us in the fire, the God we serve can rescue us from your roaring furnace, and anything else you might **cook up**, Oh king. <u>But even if He doesn't, it wouldn't make a bit of difference</u>, Oh king. We still wouldn't serve your gods or worship the gold statue you set up."[27] These men know where the power is. And so, should we.

---

[25] For example; Judas- Mt 26: 14-16 NIV; Peter – Mt 16: 22-23. NIV The other Gospels have similar events.

[26] See Da 3:8-18 NIV

[27] E. Peterson, Da 3:16-18, *The Message*. This version is most clear to me.

CHAPTER III
EMOTIONAL THINKING

ET Examples

Why is hummus[1] called hummus and not smashed chickpea babies? Why are hamburgers called hamburgers and not ground up cow meat patties? Sounds like an odd way to talk about food, but the reason is most likely: food companies like to disassociate the food we eat with its source. What if a spouse was accustomed to saying: "Honey, while you are at the store, pick up some smashed chickpea babies and ground up cow meat patties." Think about it. When the charged terms 'babies' and 'cow meat' reach your ears, you are more likely to have an emotional reaction to the terms. So, if you use words that are not related to the actual source of the food, there will be no emotional reaction. The chance of you buying 'smashed baby chickpeas' is remote, but hummus isn't. As a teacher I was always surprised when I asked students such questions as: 'Where does hamburger come from?" and their answer was: "the store." And then of course, some farm boy or girl would laugh and tell them where they really came from. And of course, many of the students would go 'ugh' or 'ew.'

[1] Hummus- a paste or dip made of chickpeas mashed with oil, garlic, lemon juice and tahini.

The problem is that we don't want our food mixed up with our emotions. We don't want our emotions to interfere when we are eating. This is why we are so averse to cannibalism. Eating our own kind is repulsive to us, yet under the right set of circumstance[2], you might very well find yourself being a cannibal. There are just too many emotions which include YOU, when cannibalism is discussed. If only cows could talk. Even with our animal food removed from our emotional filters[3], plant food is even more so. Why is it that animals get most our emotional concern and not plants? Are we phytophobic,[4] or just phytocides?[5] "That's easy;" you say, "animals are more like us. We can relate to them better. They have nervous systems like us and they can feel pain like us." But does that thinking make plants any less a form of miraculous life than animals? In fact, plants have been on this planet a lot longer than animals, and they will be more likely the ones that survive if we destroy ourselves with modern warfare or planetary neglect. Remember, they can make their own food, and we can't. In fact, we are totally dependent on them to make food for animals[6]. So, they really should get a great deal of our respect as far as living things go. And we have no fear of them (I've never been attacked by a plant, except maybe poison ivy). They pose no threat to us, whereas animals do, so we have some fear about animals.

It looks to me like our emotions have a lot to do with how we think about our food, and how we revere living things. The conclusion that I come up with for this situation is that all life needs to be respected and cared for. Yes, here is an A/NT that I can get behind. The other 'truth' that comes from this thinking is

---

[2] The Donner Party: a group of pioneers that spent the winter of 1846-47 snowbound; some resorting to cannibalism.

[3] How we regulate our emotions; moderating our emotions based on experience.

[4] Phyto – plant, phobic- fearful

[5] Plant killers

[6] It's called photosynthesis.

that we have the power of life and death over plants and animals in a very fundamental way, since they are our food sources. How we 'feel' about our animal and plant friends needs a revision of our ET. Is it 'wrong' or 'right' to be a vegan or meat eater? That's really a choice we make. Our emotions are what make it either 'right' or 'wrong.' Emotions can really get in the way of clear thinking.

Ebola, Radon, war, terrorism, pesticides, pollution, global climate change (warming); and list could go on and on. We live in a culture of fear. We have systematically increased the level of fear in America since World War II. If you asked your great grand-parents about Radon or terrorism or Ebola or global climate change, they would have said; "What are you talking about?" President Roosevelt said during WWII that "the only thing we have to fear is fear itself."[7] Of course he was referring to the conditions during WWII, but he was also prophetic. I remember when I was in 7th grade my social studies focused on the evils of communism and we all feared the great threat that it posed on the world at that time. But as time went on, more and more fears began to surface in our life style from the food we eat to the trust of people that were different from 'us.' Then our fears became more toward the institutions we had set up to protect and serve us. Now we fear government regulation, and inflation, and hacking of our personal information. The list of fears only seems to increase as we plunge into the future of technology and the 'information age.' This high level of fear causes many people seek refuge in blaming others in our country irrationally. We are becoming like fearful lemmings, that during the peak of their population cycle, they run in herds that run into large bodies of water, where some of them die.[8] Fear is a powerful motivator. Fear is a powerful emotional filter. And fear is a major source of confused and unclear thinking. A major ET.

---

[7] http://historymatters.edu. Franklin D. Roosevelt's first inaugural address; 3/4/1933.

[8] https://www.britannica.com/story/do-lemmings-really-commit-suicide

Another ET that gets in the way of clear thinking is summed up in the phrase that I heard often in my childhood: "What will people think of you?" I have spent a lot of emotional time in my life worrying about what other people thought of me. Not only is that pretty egotistical, but it is a waste of mental time. Since I have no control over what 'other people think' and I really have only clues about what they are thinking, it doesn't make much sense to obsess about it. But I do anyway. I have found what is helpful to me in this ET, is to tell myself: "you wouldn't care what other people thought of you, if you knew how little they did [think about me]." That gets to the egotistical part of this ET.

Then there is the ET about our pets. As of 2018, Americans owned 60 million dogs. These dogs are mostly being 'best friends' and companions on this road to life, but as usual there is a down side. Of the 10 most vicious dogs who have attacked and killed their owners and other people, the top three are the Pitbull (no surprise here), the Rottweiler, and the German Shepard. A chronological study done by Animals24-7 from 1982-2014 found that these three breeds accounted for a majority of injuries and deaths of human beings: German Shepard- 15 deaths out of 113 attacks; Rottweiler – 85 deaths out of 535 attacks; Pitbull -295 deaths out of 3,397 attacks[9]. I think the numbers speak for themselves, that obviously the most dangerous dog in American is the Pitbull. And by a big margin. So, the question arises, why do people own them and defend them and 'love' them? In my way of thinking it is emotional or ET. But what are the emotions that these folks are defending their pets for? The first one is obviously the feeling of security. These dogs make their owners feel secure. "Nobody bothers me!" This decision to have a very dangerous animal is usually based on this feeling alone. What they seem to ignore by making this ET is that when I have a Pitbull, I am subjecting the

---

[9] https://animals24-7/Dog Attacks Death and Maiming, US and Canada 1982-2018.

people who live around me to my decision. And I am disregarding their value as fellow humans. I am subjecting them to the whims of my decision to own a Pitbull, all for my feeling of security. So, in effect, I am putting my feelings over the feelings of others. But this is America, I can do what I like! So, let me use a metaphor that was used by C.S. Lewis in his book Mere Christianity.[10]"You can get the idea (of morality) plain if you think of us as a fleet of ships sailing in formation. The voyage will be a success only, in the first place, if the ships do not collide and get in one another's way; and secondly, if each ship is seaworthy and has their engines in good order. As a matter of fact, you cannot have either of these two things without the other. If the ships keep on having collisions they will not be seaworthy very long." So, in effect, C. S. Lewis is saying that we need to consider the feelings of others in this world so that we can all get to our destinations as we sail through the times of our lives. If we only think of our own feelings we will begin to collide with others more and more and then we cannot get anywhere as a group. So, if my selfish thinking (my needs, my wants, my desires) causes harm to others, (colliding with them), then there must be something in my 'engine' (brain/mind) causing the problem. And that, I submit, is ET.

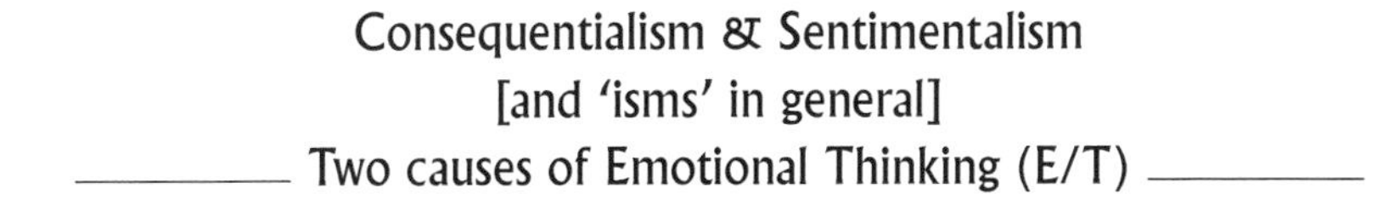

Consequentialism & Sentimentalism [and 'isms' in general] Two causes of Emotional Thinking (E/T)

Unfortunately, I will have to do something I don't like doing in order to explain what causes a destructive (in my opinion) thinking pattern I call ET. I will use two '-isms' as way of explanation: consequentialism and sentimentalism. First let me define them. Consequentialism you probably know best by the phrase; 'the ends

[10] C. S. Lewis; *Mere Christianity,* (renewed copyright 1980; HarperCollins) p. 71.

justify the means.' America has become a land of people who believe we can give the world our brand of democracy by whatever means is necessary to achieve it. We are even willing to live with a ruling oligarchy (congress) if it means achieving our ends (Life, liberty and the pursuit of happiness.) So far, no government has demonstrated its ability to move history in the direction it wants it to go. But that doesn't keep us from trying. Many 'Christians' are of this opinion and join political parties to help America achieve its goals, by attempting to sway these parties more and more toward their religious agendas, which they think is what "Christians" should do to make America more and more "Christian."

This idea of consequentialism fits in nicely with the other 'ism;' sentimentalism. Sentimentalism[11]is when we believe that if we **feel good** about doing something that we consider moral, then it must be the right thing to do. Some slogans you might hear from a sentimentalist is: "If it feels right, do it." Or; "Just follow your heart/feelings." Or as an excuse: "I was just trying to be nice." Notice that the whole axiom is a feeling about a moral stand. Probably, in my way of thinking the most abused term in relation to sentimentalism is love. Now here is a truly emotional term for those who are sentimentalists. Love, for them, is a feeling. I think the Greeks had it right on love. Instead of using just one term they used 4: family love (storge), love of friends (philia), romantic love (eros), and unconditional/divine love (agape). For me, the only ones that are purely emotional are Eros and storge. These both illicit some pretty strong feelings. But as a Follower of Jesus what I strive for is AGAPE. Now occasionally you will 'feel' good about doing agape things, but in general your feelings when loving in the agape form aren't around. As when Jesus asks us to love our enemies. So, if we are looking for warm comfy feelings when we do agape love, we will be sadly mistaken. So, then for me real love (agape – which can include all the others) is an ACT and not a FEELING. This also

[11] Sometimes called Moral Sense Theory

means that I can love someone without liking them. When I think this way, I am on the road to learning to love my enemies.

Now for 'isms' in general. When the suffix 'ism' is placed on a word, it usually is a way to define a belief system of some sort. For example; theism, atheism, agnosticism, deism, pantheism, etc. And you could probably fill up a book with all the different 'isms' there are. Another way to look at 'isms' is that they represent the mental 'filters' or 'lenses' that people look at the world through. These belief systems called 'isms' are words we use to define in a 'nutshell' what beliefs we have. The other significant thing about 'isms' for me is that they are usually based on some emotional 'filter' or 'lens' as well. Again, it would take a book to describe all the emotional 'filters' that are used to decide which 'ism' you choose to belong to. You have to remember that the brain has at least as much circuitry for emotion as it does for the higher intellectual skills, like reason and logic, and reflection, etc. That is just the way we are wired. Ideas have to pass through our emotional 'filters' before they can be subjected to the higher thinking skills. This is the reason why our limbic system[12], the seat of our emotions is considered to be a more 'primitive' part of the brain, having evolved earlier than the cerebrum.[13]

Cuteness

There is a science of 'cuteness.'[14] It seems that evolution has 'tricked' us into liking our offspring by causing a pleasure response in our pleasure center called the nucleus accumbens.[15] And in addition it makes sure we remember this cuteness by honing a chemical memory in our amygdala. This obviously improves our

[12] Part of the brain below the cerebrum

[13] The part of the brain containing the two cerebral hemispheres, the largest part of the human brain.

[14] http://blogs.unimelb.edu.au/sciencecommunication/2013/08/26

[15] A ganglion in the basal forebrain known as the 'reward circuit.'

baby's chance of survival. You might know that some animals have to protect the babies from their fathers because the fathers will eat them. This 'cuteness' response also helps make sure that our offspring are not ignored by their parents (we seem to have a lot of people ignoring their kids anyway). If you have ever witnessed a family 'gushing' over a new born offspring, you know how 'cuteness' affects them. Evidently our babies did not evolve to be cute, we evolved to 'think' babies are cute. When you see big round eyes, small noses, soft round bodies (hair is soft), and large heads, our pleasure center is activated. And the more 'cute' the stronger the reaction, and the reaction is reinforced by the amygdala. Obviously, this is a type of emotional thinking (ET). The problem comes when we don't realize that this is what is happening to us.

'Cuteness' is a problem when we make decisions based on this highly emotional response to soft, round stuff. Again, going through life unaware of how these emotions rule our decisions. We are sold stuff based on this reaction. Not only does sex sell, 'cuteness' sells too. Have you noticed how many ads have cute kids, puppies, etc.? They want your money and these ads know how 'cuteness' **effects and affects** YOU.

One other idea that relates to 'cuteness' is the bouba/kiki effect. What? This is a study that was done in 2001 by V. Ramachandan,[16] who did a study using diagrams that were either sharp and pointy or round and curvy. He asked his American subjects to describe the diagrams as either 'bouba' or 'kiki' (made up words). Ninety eight percent described the sharp pointy diagrams as 'kiki' and ninety five percent described the round curvy diagrams as 'bouba.' Ramachandan explained this effect by the way we pronounce words; when we say 'bouba' the mouth produces a rounded effect (when you say it your lips become rounded). Is it possible that even our language is affected by our 'cuteness' response? This study

[16] Neuroscientist at University of California

certainly suggests something is going on in our brains about how we perceive our world when we name things.

I think that cuteness interferes with our ability to see beauty. But, what is beauty? Almost everyone has heard the expression: "Beauty is in the eye of the beholder."[17] So, beauty is a subjective thing that is much broader than 'cuteness.' Beauty also includes such emotions as satisfaction, a sense of balance and harmony. If we are emotionally hijacked by 'cuteness,' beauty can (unfortunately) be included and limit our experience of beauty. To some people, 'cuteness' is beauty. When you take that emotional position, you are not able to see the beauty in a reptile, or frog, or the beauty of a mind, or the Lord, pine needles, wrinkled old people, mathematical equations, laws of the universe, and just plain old 'being' itself. I think the ultimate objective of beauty is to 'see' all of creation as beautiful. So, let your higher brain centers rule! Broaden your sense of beauty. See a snake for real. They really are beautifully 'cute.'

"I'm Right!"

Because God has chosen to endow our brains with many emotional circuits that continuously monitor our thought, we become easy prey to our emotions as we try to think through the issues of our lives. Tantamount to our thinking skills, our emotions vie for rule of our conscious lives. Too much of the time we give in to them and let our emotions take us to false and often destructive conclusions about these issues that we are trying to solve.

Feeling good about ourselves is a crucial part to our well-being and feelings of self-worth. Very often we learn in school and with others that being right can endow our emotions with feelings of self-worth, as if by being right that makes us worth more. The truth is that we are all worth a huge amount in the eyes of God

[17] First appeared in 3rd century BC in Greek

and rightly thinking people, regardless of being right or wrong. I have been wrong many times in my married life, but my wife still loves me and sees me as a person of great intelligence and worth. Now that is true love!

The danger again, is that being right can be used as a form of emotional blackmail, as can money and being lucky. The more I depend on my sense of "being right", the more I begin to crave the feelings that go along with it, and more and more I am willing to defend my positions of "rightness" regardless of whether they are correct or not. I begin to use my friend rationalization in order to build the fortress of rightness that I need to continue to massage my self-worth through the need to be right.

Look around. The world of the internet is full of blogs and opinion web sites that all need to be right. Pure un-slanted news is hard to find! Churches are brimming with self-proclaimed tellers of their own personal brands of truth, selecting biblical texts that suit their own need to be right, and neglecting any contrary texts that might counter their truth claims. Again, the danger of this need to be right is very polarizing. Where are the clear thinkers? Where is humility and the sense that your ideas and opinions are just as important as mine?

Case in point: In the small town where I live there are two ways to go thru town. One is the main highway and the other is to use a back road that has two stop signs. When we first moved into this town, I tried both ways and found that the main road is just as fast as the back road with two stop signs, and most of the time the main road was quicker. Several times coming home thru town I have seen cars behind me use the back road and then I pass them at the stop sign and they are right behind me again. No gain. One time I did this and smiled at the guy at the stop sign. He saw that as me being right and him wrong. So, when he got up the hill out of town he passed me as soon as he could. As if to say: There, "I'm ahead of you anyway. I'm right and you're wrong!" (and I'll risk my life to be right!) This to me demonstrates the power of the need to be right. Somehow the need to be right enrages many people and they then act very irrationally. Again, the ugly face of pride shows up to rule in our lives. And I should not have smiled at him. That was my sense of wanting to be right.

Which brings me to the idea of sovereignty. A sovereign is a person who has supreme power or authority and sovereignty is the state of having that power/authority. Nations like to think they are sovereign. Kings and queens and dictators like to think they are sovereign. In my mind they are not sovereign. Only God is sovereign. So, what does this have to do with being right? Well, a lot. There are a lot of people who think that what they believe is sovereign. And that is a result of the culture that they have been brought up in. We Americans have been trained from the time we were born to decide what is 'best' for ourselves. What is 'best' for us to wear, or eat, or our hair cut, or what career to choose, what colleges, what kind of car, and the list of 'bests' for us goes on and on. So, by the time we become adults we 'know' what is 'best' for us. So then, when it comes to what is 'best' for me, I am sovereign. I am the supreme power of my wants and my needs and my feelings. And this is what Peterson calls the "holy trinity of self.[18]" This supreme authority that we learn early in life is most often expressed in our need to be right. "How dare someone question what I know is right!" "Who do they think they are?!" "Don't they know I know what is best for me (and therefore 'right')?" This is another form of pride and narcissism. Humility takes a back seat as we cry "me, me, me," into the night.

[18] E. Peterson; *Eat This Book*; Eerdmans Publishing Co.; p. 33. 2006.

Eat, Drink, and be Merry...

"Eat, drink and be merry for tomorrow you may die."[19] This is the slogan of the people with no hope. This is the mantra of the 'materialist.' A 'materialist' is a person who doesn't think there is anything more to life than what can be sensed through our at least 9 physical senses. Also, there are our senses of hunger, thirst, etc., which describe our 'needs.'[20] And then there are the sense of time, or agency, and I could go on. But, my point is that the 'materialist' thinks that this is all there is to life. There is no 'spiritual' in our lives. Remember that 'spiritual' refers to the metaphysical; whatever lies beyond the realm of the physical. 'Materialists' believe that this realm does not exist, and therefore, God, being a Spirit, does not exist. Many scientists are 'materialists' as well as some philosophers and people who call themselves 'realists.'

People who have hope are people who believe that this life has meaning beyond our physical being. These are people who the 'materialists' call 'believers.' When I have been engaged in a discussion with a 'materialist' and I talk about my belief in God, I can see their nonverbals become decidedly distrustful of my thinking. Sometimes they ask if I am going to try to 'convert' them. But I am not. They are entitled to believe whatever they choose. What I don't like is when these 'materialists' tell me that my beliefs are inferior to theirs. My point is that they don't know if this physical life is all that there is and neither do I. Neither one of us can 'prove' our beliefs one way or the other.

'Eat, drink and be merry' is a slogan that in my opinion is based on emotions. Here is how I think it plays out emotionally: I am going to die and become nothing, therefore I have to grab all the 'good' things in life so I can enjoy them before I die, because

[19] This is a fusion of Ecc 8:15 and Isa 22:13. NIV

[20] See Maslow's hierarchy of needs; https//www.learning-theories.com/maslows-heirarchy-of-needs.html

this is all there is. Poor me, I better enjoy all I can now, and get my wants and needs met NOW! The emotion is fear.

The person who believes there is more than this physical life, has hope. The dictionary defines hope as feeling that 'things' will turn out for the best. And I think hope is related to the idea that these 'things' in life will be set straight. A kind of 'justice' for the universe will take place.[21]

Materialism is a very enticing 'ism.' Our bodies are set to a particle mode. What I mean by that is our senses communicate the world around us through the detection of particles. Those particles being vibrating molecules (sound), or photons of light (sight), or aromatic molecules (smell and taste), or texture/shape of molecules (touch). A very 'materialistic' ability (our senses). We can easily become seduced by our senses into believing that this particle world is all that there is. Therefore, you will hear materialists say: "If you can't measure it, it doesn't exist." Notice the A/NT thinking here. Possibilities have been limited to what is sensed and then assumed to be 'reality.' So, any experiences that I have that are not entirely sensed, are not real. As Scrooge said in A Christmas Carol: "It's humbug still! I won't believe it.[22]" (after experiencing a hallucination or two). Clearly Scrooge has been a materialist all his life; until he has an experience that is not in the realm of his senses. Yes, this is a fictional story, but I believe that most people have experiences that are not in the realm of their senses, they just don't know what to do with them. For example; if you 'sense' sweetness when you read a text; or depth when you hear a voice; or a 'feeling' of being at home and comfortable when you converse with a friend; what does this 'sensing' mean? And more importantly, what do they reveal about the world and universe around us? You may just be beginning to understand that there is more to the world than our senses reveal. There is a depth and

[21] See section of this book on word problems; p.41

[22] C. Dickens, *A Christmas Carol,* (Chapman & Hall, London 1843) p. 13.

meaning in the patterns of relationships that we have with each other and the created order around us.

Science has revealed to us a world of waves and fields.[23] For example, a magnetic field is all around a magnet, but you can't see it unless you put iron filings around the magnet and then the magnetic field is visible. We have instruments that detect these waves and fields, like a spectroscope, or magnetometer, or (are you ready) a Laser Interferometer! But the point that I want to make is that these instruments change the un-sensed nature of fields and waves into a particle mode so that we can 'see' them or 'show' mathematically of their existence. So, I guess, if you think that all that there is are what you sense, then that must be a false assumption.

But, what if there is a whole realm of being that is beyond our senses? Over the last several millennia, we have called this possibility metaphysical, or spiritual. That is, a realm of being that cannot be sensed but can be known, by our cache of unexplained experiences. In my life, these unexplained experiences have produced a pattern of meaning that has taken on more and more shape, texture and completeness as I have aged.

So then, we have a basic decision to make in our lives. Is there a spiritual realm or not? What you decide here makes the difference in whether you believe in God or not. The Bible says that "God is Spirit."[24] But in order for you to believe that, you need to believe in a spiritual realm.

---

[23] Wave – a disturbance that transfers energy through space or matter, with little or no associated mass transport. Field – (quantum theory); occupies space, contains energy, and it is present in a true vacuum; i.e.- electromagnetic field.

[24] Jn 4:24a; NIV

BOBO
(Brain On Back Order)

Some people just don't like to think. They 'think' that thinking is too difficult, tiresome, and painful (they might just have to ignore some of their desired feelings). Even better for these folks is that they want their thinking to match their feelings. Then the thinking becomes minimal and we just do what feels good to us. This process takes a lot of guesswork out of decision making. Some slogans you hear are these: "just do it." "If it feels good, do it." "Eat your feelings[25]" "Taste the feeling"[26] "I have mixed drinks about feelings." And then there are those that add A/NT to the mix: "Respect people's feelings even if it doesn't mean anything to you, it could mean everything to them." Everything? I think you get my point.

People who let their feelings be their guide through life are what I have termed BOBO (Brain On Back Order). I think that is a much better term than 'brain dead' because their brains are not really dead, just out of service, and a 'nice' way to describe them is that they just choose not to use their brain. And BOBO is a nice acronym to remember. But they could 'reorder' their brain and put thinking back into their routines.

Of course, there are differing degrees of BOBOs, just as with most complex behaviors in life, this phenomenon is a continuum (if you are a confirmed BOBO reading this book, a highly unlikely event, then there is hope! Read on!).

---

[25] Urban Dictionary; https://www.urbandictionary.com

[26] Coca-Cola ad; https://www.coca-cola.ie/stories/taste-the-feeling

BOBOs Among Us[27]

I live among the BOBOs
I see their legions grow.
I live among them in a most cautious state,
Knowing that at any time
They can seal my fate.
They drive their cars,
Their cell phones active.
(They think that this is most attractive.)
They look not where their cars may lead.
They talk as they drive,
Not aware of their speed.
When driving their cars,
They follow to near.
Their glazed expressions
Show no fear.

They drive to fast when they need to go slow,
They drive too slow when it starts to snow.
They pause on a hill when the weather's severe
No knowledge of physics,
They stay in high gear.

They hurry here,
They hurry there.
Why they rush
They do not care.

In the fog their cars have no lights.
They only use them in the night.

[27] D. Poole; 2010. In the style of Dr. Seuss.

They wander the shopping malls
Like in a fog.
They don't see you coming
They stop like a log.
You weave right
You weave left,
But neither will do,
They just blink and stare at you.
You are just an object
That's slightly off-sync
You might as well be a kitchen sink!
They love 'power shopping'
And 'make-up' swapping,
(And brain lobe lopping?)
When they seek knowledge,
It's really their dread.
(there's really not much going on in their head)
They suck up statistics as if they are true
And shun the hard work of thought
They must do.
Demeaning the gift
They have tween their ears,
They seek the easy life
With gusto and cheers.
Their lack of awareness
Is their greatest sin.
They miss all the wonder;
(no thoughts coming in)
They miss the Mystery of life;
They'd rather spend their time sharpening a knife.

My attempt here is to improve the thinking skills of our culture, particularly our youth. I am tired and angry at all the destructive, senseless behaviors that I see and hear about. As Socrates said so long ago: "There is nothing new under the sun." I don't believe that today's youth are much different than the many generations before them. The only difference I see is in the quantity of events, that seem to be on the rise. The social media sites only seem to amplify the effect of this BOBO behavior.

Our school systems have gone astray. They think: "Maybe if we hand out contraceptives, teens won't get pregnant. Maybe if we teach sex education more thoroughly, teens won't get pregnant. Maybe if we teach more about drugs, teens won't take drugs. Maybe if we teach more about bullying students won't be bullies." And the list of ills and remedies goes on. What really will handle all these ills is if we begin again to teach students how to think. I don't mean a course slapped into the curriculum in the senior year of high school. I mean an on-going continuous thread of learning starting with Kindergarten and woven continuously through the senior year of high school. What are the thinking skills needed to decide about sexual behavior, drug abuse, aggressive behavior, etc.? The first step is to understand the thinking or lack of thinking that is present in today's teens and them to design a K-12[28] course that will address those needs.

[28] Kindergarten through the senior year in high school.

CHAPTER IV

ANTHROPOMORPHIC THINKING

AT Examples

First, I need to say that this thinking pattern is the **least destructive** of the three that I have identified. I believe it is a subset of emotional thinking. I have set it apart from ET because many people are very sensitive to their feelings for animals. Still, I think it needs to be addressed for the following reason. The American culture spends an inordinate amount of money on their pets. This is hard for me to justify when there are literally millions of people around the world going hungry and without proper health care every day. According to American Pet Products Association[1] Americans spent 69.1 billion dollars on their pets and that is expected to rise to 72.1 billion dollars in 2018. Most of this spending is on pet food, which has become more and more expensive due to 'premium' food options. The category of health care for pets has increased the most in cost to about 7% (17.1 – 18.2 billion dollars) in the last two years. By comparison, America spends 42.4 billion (2017) on foreign aid, which includes building armies in other countries.

[1] Press release from American Pet Products Association 3/22/2018; https://prnewswire.com/news-releases

That is less than 1% of our government's budget![2] This is just to give you a perspective. The amount we spend on humanitarian efforts around the globe is even less. So, my observation that we need to reign in our inordinate animal 'feelings' seems to be pretty accurate. There is a Bible verse which comes to mind: "If anyone has material possessions and sees a brother or sister in need but has no pity on them, how can the love of God be in that person?[3]" And then of course the obvious question: Who are my brothers and sisters? How narrow do you define that question? I think you get my point.

I first remember when I was about 7 years of age, my sister took me to the movies to see Bambi. This was the first movie I remember that I heard and saw animals talk. And they had feelings just like mine. Of course, the trauma for me and other children at the time was that Bambi's mom gets killed by hunters. And right when you were identifying with Bambi and thought his mom was a good mom. Now I realize how easy it is for children to put their feelings into animals. Of course, it's a short mental 'hike' to continue this practice of putting our feelings into animals as we get older. Some people never stop doing this and the result is AT (Anthropomorphic Thinking). As usual, some of the time these AT thinkers don't even know they are doing it, since it has been a pattern of thinking for them since childhood. And just like the other two thinking patterns I am describing, it can become an unconscious process.

Back in November 2015, I heard an ad for pet food. The opening line was "The cats are a part of our family like our kids."[4] Really? How is that possible? Do they share the same genetics? What does that comment mean? Or more importantly, what does the pet food company want us to think it means? What does this say about

---

[2] The U.S. foreign aid budget visualized, https://www.washingtonpost.com/graphics/world/which-countries-get-the-most-foreign-aid

[3] 1 Jn3:17. NIV

[4] I am not sure it's a good idea to credit the source of this comment.

our American culture and pets? When did our pets gain the same status as our children? In my way of thinking this is a form of AT. We place our nurturing feelings and behaviors on our pets, as if they were our children, thinking that our cats and dogs will love us just as our children will.

Now, I don't want you to think that I don't love animals. I do. I loved my first dog, Toby. He was my friend and he and I spent a lot of time together until I was married. Then he rejected me, and I don't blame him. I choose my wife over him. So, I am an animal lover. But, and I think you know what I mean when I say BUT. But, we need to keep our feelings about our animals at a distance. We don't know what they are thinking, and we can't assume they think like us. And that is the problem with AT thinking: thinking that they think like us. They don't.

Further, you can get bogged down in terms in regard to AT. When you try to determine the degree of 'consciousness' of animals and compare their 'consciousness' to ours, you can get totally confused. You will be wading into the terminology of many differing philosophies about animals and how or if they think like we do. In my mind, what it seems to boil down to is whether animals have self-consciousness or not. In other words, do they observe what is happening to them as it is happening. I know that I have a mental function that observes as things happen in my life. Some people have called this function 'transcendence',[5] or 'the Adult',[6] or other terminology that show our ability to self-observe and reflect. Whether animals have this ability or not we don't know because we can't directly converse with animals and find out. We have taught chimpanzees a two-year old's vocabulary, but so far, no in-depth conversations have happened. What remains

[5] Jean-Paul Sarte (philosopher).

[6] Popularized in the 1970's (Transactional Analysis; Eric Berne). That part of our 'psyche' which observes objectively. See https://en.wikipedia.org/wiki/Transactional-analysis

is our 'wish' that they think like we do. And that 'wish' is what I think a lot of our AT comes from.

There is a principle in psychiatry called 'transference.' This was first defined by Sigmund Freud.[7] Basically it means that when someone is in therapy they transfer their feelings about their father/mother/sibling on to their therapist or someone else meaningful to them. The key here for me is the **transfer of feelings,** because I think that is what we do when we are in AT. As, the following example shows, this can be destructive: In Africa there was a black rhinoceros male that was attacking and killing young black rhinos and female rhinos, a general threat to the endangered species status that these rhinoceroses enjoyed. So, a branch of the Namibian government gave a Texas hunting club the right to hold a raffle to come to Namibia and kill this rogue rhino. When the media caught wind of this, a nightmare for the 'winner' of the raffle ensued. This hunter received 'death threats' and all sorts of threats on his phone and email account[8]. And here is where AT comes into the story. People would be willing to kill another human because they have won a raffle (approved by both our own fish and wildlife service, and the Namibia government) so that a rogue rhino can be 'free.' These 'death threats' are coming from people who, in my opinion, have AT running rampant in their minds, so that when it comes to the value of animals or humans, the animals have greater importance than humans. Does that raise a 'red flag' for you? It does for me.

[7] Neurologist and founder of psychoanalysis; 1856-1939.

[8] https://inhabit.com/controverial-texas-hunter-bags-his-350000-endangered-black-rhino/

Dominion or Transcendence?

There is a word that is used in the book of Genesis that needs to be changed to a better translation than the one that we all are 'used to.' That word is 'dominion.' When we read the text from Genesis; "Then God said: "Let us make man in our image, in our likeness, and let them have dominion (or' rule' depending on the translation) over the fish of the sea and the birds of the air, over the livestock, over all the earth, and over all the creatures that move along the ground.[9]" That pretty much gives us the right to 'rule' over the earth. Unfortunately, many people have taken this to mean that we can do whatever we want to the earth and its animals, since God said that we could. Boy is that ever wrong thinking. And that is why the translation of the Hebrew for 'dominion/rule' needs to be changed. The Hebrew word for 'rule' or 'dominion' in Genesis is 'radah.' This word is not the one normally used for rule in other parts of the Bible. But this word is used again in Ezekiel 34:1-6 (NIV) as to what bad 'radah' is. In verses one through six Ezekiel describes how the 'shepherds of Israel' have done a poor job ruling over the sheep of Israel. It is clear from these usages that what was meant in Genesis is that we are to care for our planet and the living things in it. We 'rule' by care and stewardship, not by getting all we can and discarding the remains as pollution and extinction.

I have been seeking a thread of thought for many, many years that has only recently become clear to me. It was initiated by the phrase from Genesis; "So God created man in his own image, in the image of God he created him."[10] First of all, this sounds like a rather 'sexist' phrase, excluding women, but don't put on your modern mind so quickly. Remember when and in what context this was written. Secondly, notice the repetition of the 'creating in His image' part. Repetition is used in the Old Testament to make a

---

[9] Ge 1:26 NIV

[10] Ge 1:27 NIV

point. We humans are the 'image bearers' on this earth. We are the only ones. It is our 'vocation' to be 'image bearers.' As N.T. Wright so eloquently put it: "...reflecting the Creator's wise stewardship into the world and reflecting the praises of all creation back to its maker. Those who do so are the "royal priesthood" the "kingdom of priests," the people who are called to stand at the dangerous but exhilarating point where heaven and earth meet.[11]" So, you see, the stewardship of the 'image bearers' is our vocation and purpose. Our morality is not all that we need to do this. We need to give up our worldly idols and worship God alone. And what idols do we continue to swear our allegiance to? The governments and huge corporations of this world, or the money of this world, or power of this world, or the 'entertainers' (sports/media stars), and of course the gods of security that we all love so much. These false gods enslave us and will lead us to our destruction.

But then there is the 'lamed.'[12] What does this letter have to do with dominion or transcendence? This letter is used in Genesis; "the Lord God formed the man from the dust of the ground and breathed into his nostrils the breath of life, and man became a living being."[13] What is omitted when this verse is translated into English is the Hebrew letter 'lamed.' This letter is often seen as the preposition 'to.' So, what? Well, if you put the word 'to' into the phrase then it reads "and man became to a living being." Again, so, what? Well to Hebrew scholars this represents a 'hint' that suggests that man has been created from a lower to higher form of existence when humans evolved. And further, Onkelos,[14] thought that this should be translated as "and the Adam (man) became a speaking

[11] N. T. Wright; *The Day the Revolution Began;* (HarperOne 2016) p.76

[12] The twelfth letter of the Hebrew alphabet; lambda in Greek, L in Latin.

[13] Ge 2:7 NIV. *The Message* version is: "God formed man out of the dirt of the ground and blew into his nostrils the breath of life; the man came alive – a living soul."

[14] A Roman national who converted to Judaism; contributor to the Talmud; 1900 years ago.

spirit." Again, so what? Well if this is the better translation then it shifts who we are as humans from- animal with a lot of spiritual possibilities to a spiritual being with a lot of animal possibilities. It means to me we have ascendancy over the animals and not dominance or 'rule' over them.

But allow me to 'unpack' ascendancy a little more. We are ascendant FROM the animals, and we have a lot of animal tendencies in us. We have duties to the animals that they do not acknowledge to us. We must care for them and respect them even if they do not respect us. If we look like prey, they will eat us. Sharkness, bear-ness, and lion-ness[15], etc., is their natural inclinations. We can train them in a manner that pleases a crowd, but their basic instincts remain. All too often we have animal trainers being attacked by their 'trained' wild animals. Again, what has gone amiss is our AT, not the animals. We need to re-think our thinking about animals and our relationship to them. We are not just another animal, but an ascended animal, to whom God has given abilities the animals do not have.

One of these abilities is the 'technology' of language. We are so used to this technology, that we don't even think of it as a technology. Yet language is our primary technology of ascendancy that God has developed through evolution.[16] Animals have language, but it is not even close to the 'technology' of language that we have developed. This 'technology' has allowed us to become more and more capable of higher thought and 'spiritual' development. We take this for granted. But this is why St. John starts his gospel book with: "In the beginning was the Word, and the Word was with God, and the Word was God.[17]" The Word is the 'language' of God. And we are privileged to receive it as ascended animals, who are spiritually equipped to hear the Word.

---

[15] Sharks will be sharks, bears will be bears, lions will be lions.

[16] Yes, animals have rudimentary 'languages,' but nothing they have compares to ours in complexity and nuance.

[17] Jn 1:1 NIV

Of all the gifts that God has given us, we take language the most for granted. Yet it is words that formed the universe. Words, not in our language, which created with the phrase "Let There Be..."[18] All the language of God that was needed for an action -LET to form entities-BE- in a space -THERE (the universe). So then, could that quantum mechanics[19] which science has discovered be the alphabet soup of creation?

[18] Ge 1:3a,6a,14a. and variations in Ge 1:9a,11a,20a,24a. NIV

[19] Quantum mechanics – the science of the very small world of sub-atomic particles, atoms and energy waves and fields.

CHAPTER V

SEEKING HIGHER TRUTH

Seeing for Real

Can You See?
The bud and bloom in the fruit?
The boy and man in the grandfather?
The girl and woman in the grandmother?
The root, stem, branch and leaf in the tree of winter?

Do you see for real?
Or only in parts?
In representations of reality;
In computer screens
And video games?

Is your vision transformed,
Or only complete?

Empty yourself into the world
With a generous spirit
And you will be free!
(after all, you are His child.)[1]

[1] D. Poole; 2017

My poem on seeing for real begins the process of understanding what it means to 'see for real.' Seeing for real involves our ability to let go. To let go of our need to separate the world into chunks of information so we can analyze it or decontextualize it. Seeing for real is our ability to see without prejudice or A/NT. Seeing for real involves our ability to see and hear subtleties that are sensed and not known through logic. Whole-brain thinkers intuitively know this. Another quote which comes to mind is from William Blake's poem 'The Everlasting Gospel:' "This life's five windows of the soul distorts the heavens from pole to pole. And leads you to believe a lie, when you see with not through the eye.[2]" Here Blake contrasts the prepositions 'with' and 'through.' *With* implies that we are using the eye as a tool and *through* implies that we are passive, not making judgements as we see. In other words, we let our eyes see the subtleties of the world around us, not jumping to conclusions as our A/NT would have us do. This idea also reinforces what Jesus said about seeing and hearing. "This is why I speak to them in parables: Though seeing, they do not see; though hearing, they do not hear or understand.[3]" My take on this is that Jesus is telling us to 'see' and 'hear' the subtleties around us. Don't make snap judgements about what you 'see' or 'hear.' Jesus reinforced His view in many of the stories of the New Testament. One that comes to mind is the story in the book of John about Jesus and the Samaritan woman at the well (John 4:1-26 NIV). In this story Jesus sees the woman for real. He picks up on subtleties that are not obvious if you're not seeing for real. For example, the fact that the woman is coming to the well for water at noon, when all the other women have already left is a clue about her life. She is a divorced woman, who the other women shun. This is revealed later in the story. And again, Jesus sees for real when a woman came to one of the Pharisee's house and washed Jesus' feet with her hair

---

[2] https://bartelby.com/236/58.html (public domain)

[3] Mt 13:13 NIV

and poured expensive perfume on them. The Pharisee disapproved of this act and Jesus used this event as a teaching moment about forgiveness. But then Jesus says: "Do you see this woman?[4]" The Pharisee in this story did not see for real, he only perceived her as a 'sinner.' Jesus saw this woman for real; a woman who loved God and needed forgiveness. The Pharisee decided based on his A/NT and did not see for real. If you read the stories in the New Testament carefully you will find many more examples of Jesus seeing for real.

As followers of Jesus we must learn to see for real in order to have the "mind of Christ.[5]" This 'mind' of Christ is one that sees for real, suspending judgement, until most of the 'facts' are in. This also is a 'mind' of humility. We stand before the universe in awe and mystery, not jumping to conclusions about what we see and hear.

There is a song by Brandon Heath that has a chorus that begins: "Give me Your eyes for just one second. Give me Your eyes so I can see, Everything, that I keep missing...[6]" Well here's a start:

Can you begin to see as God sees?

Can you see the billions upon billions of chloroplasts cycling almost perpetually as the warming sun mobilizes them? Can you see the rigid structures of cellulose providing their homes of protection, or the countless water molecules vibrating, connecting and wobbling in their polar bonds? God sees all these things at every moment in time.

Can you begin to see as God sees?

The billions upon billions of stones, rocks, magma, crystals, vibrating with various degrees of energy as they release and absorb radiant and electromagnetic energy? Or do you see the microscopic dances of electrons in their orbits; or the lattices of crystals and

---

[4] Lk 7:44 NIV

[5] Ph 2:5 NIV

[6] https://www.azlyrics.com/lyrics/brandonheath/givemeyoureyes.html

minerals; or the free electrons sliding across the surfaces of metals and rushing over wires? God does at every moment in time.

Can you begin to see as God sees?

The billions of cells that make up each one of the billions of humans with their arrays of microtubules, intercellular structures, gated membranes and myriad enzymes interacting, replicating, and coordinating so that we can think and be? Can you sense the wonder and sheer awesomeness of who you are? God does and He rejoices in that created goodness.

God is much greater than we can or ever begin to imagine. Not only does He know ever hair on you head, but He knows every disulfide bond and keratin molecule in each strand of that hair. He knows where every electron is going in every ATP[7] or on every "smart" phone to power our craving for 'knowing' something to sate our 'simplest' need. He is the source and ground in all being. He is the beginning and the end. The Alpha and Omega. He simply is. He is the great I AM.

There is a higher order of things only alluded to in our scriptures and theoretical minds. But that higher order is not to be found in "memes" or "multiverse." These are inventions of the human mind to explain what it cannot begin to explain: The Mystery.

'Seeing for real' involves our need to understand just how much God loves us. We will not ever fully understand the love that God has for each and every one of us. We are too finite. The most complete and concrete example of God's love for us is the cross of Christ. It is at the cross that we begin to 'see for real' the love of God for each one of us. Here is where we find our light, the radiant Truth. The eyes of the flesh cannot see this open Word, only the eyes of the mind and heart, rejoicing together in what they have 'seen for real.'

---

[7] See list of abbreviations at the end of this book.

Singularities

A singularity is an event that only happens once. There are two types that I can distinguish. 1) A once in a universe event that alters the shared history of the universe. 2) A 'common' singularity: for example, you and I are 'once in a universe' events, or as the song goes: "There will never be another you.[8]" Also, in a strict sense, since time is continually passing by, each event is unique in its time stamp, so unless you have many events happening simultaneously (and there are a huge number of events happening simultaneously) then the events in one individual's life are singularities themselves. So, you 'see,' you are by definition a 'common' singularity!

But I want to focus on is what I consider universe changing singularities. These are singularities we all share. 1) the beginning of the universe; 2) the beginning of life; 3) the creation/evolution of humans; 4) the Christ event. Remember that I am writing from a 'Christian' standpoint, so the last two universe events (Humans and Christ) are more significant to me. You may perceive a different set of universe changing singularities than me. But I think we can agree on the first two. All four of my universe changing singularities have been studied in great detail, but the circumstances surrounding each of these events remain unknown. It's like reaching a goal by going half the distance each time we try. We can get very close to the event, but we don't get there. Like the old joke goes: There was a psychologist who wanted to study the difference between male mathematicians and scientists. He lined up a group of women along a wall and told the male mathematicians and scientists that they could hug the women when they got to them, but they could only go half the distance to them at a time. Well, the mathematicians threw up their hands and left, since they knew that they would not get to the women

[8] M. Gordon, "There Will Never be Another You," https://secoondhandsongs.com/work/7818

going half the distance at a time (there would always be half a distance to go), but the scientists knew they could get close enough 'for practical purposes.' This joke is like these universes changing singularities that we have in common, we can get close to them, but we are not sure of the circumstances in which they occurred.

As a Follower of Jesus, another universe changing singularity for me is the "Christ Event."[9] In my way of thinking this 'event' changed the very nature of the universe we live in. First of all, if you are a believer in the scriptures of the New Testament, you will notice that the life and death of this Jesus of Nazareth are filled with 'cosmic'[10] events. At his birth there are signs in the 'heavens' (star of Bethlehem). At His death there are earthquakes and darkness.[11] This "Christ Event" is cloaked in mystery. We either believe it or we don't. But remember, the Big Bang and the origin of life are cloaked in mystery too. What I mean by mystery is 'hidden' from our understanding.

Karl Rahner[12] believed that it was the very nature of matter to develop into 'spirit.' Gerald Schroeder[13] says that we are a 'speaking spirit.' God has been evolving matter into greater and greater complexities, and matter has become more and more 'conscious,' culminating in us. And we are the first 'conscious' beings capable of a relationship with our Creator. Then when this singularity called the "Christ Event" flashes a message to us, do we 'get it,' or do we just ignore it, or say that since it can't be proven, it didn't happen? And that is the problem with a once in a universe singularity.

I can't express enough the role that uncertainty plays in our lives. I know, that is a tough pill to swallow, particularly those of us who have chosen to think out of our left-brains. Uncertainty

---

[9] This, for me is the birth, life, crucifixion, and resurrection of Jesus the Christ.

[10] Cosmic: anything pertaining to the cosmos [universe].

[11] Mt 27:51; Lk 23:44. NIV

[12] Roman Catholic theologian of the 20th century.

[13] An orthodox Jewish physicist; see annotated bibliography #7

is abhorrent to many people. We like things to be predictable and certain. Singularities violate that predictability that we like so much. For example, the greatest degree of certainty can be obtained in the study of mathematics. We can be very sure that 2 + 2 = 4, if we are using the common number system that we use every day. Quantification is the most certain idea that we have going for us in the modern world and we are very good at it. Most science is based on the accumulation of 'data' (quantities) and the inferences that this data can tell us. Singularities are not certainties. This immediately puts us in the realm of the right-brain, which handles uncertainties a lot better than our left-brain. Uncertainty is the source of much fear in our culture. Particularly things we can't sense like Radon and X-rays and microwaves and spyware and malware and 'cookies' and bots (if you get my drift).

But it is singularities that provide for us a 'window' or 'door' into wonder. It is when we realize that there are a lot of uncertainty in the universe that we can access our sense of wonder. Singularities help us to revive our sense of mystery. They ground our sense of being. And then there is the greatest of all singularities; unproven, mysterious, and ONE. GOD. And this one is not a number.

What is Information?
Is information embedded in the fabric of the universe?

"He is the image of the invisible God, the firstborn over all creation. For by him all things were created, things in heaven and on earth, visible and invisible, whether thrones or powers or rulers or authorities. All things were created by Him for Him.[14]" Let me 'unpack' these two verses in relation to modern science, if you will. When science uncovered the quantum world, I think the most honest response would have been; "What in the universe is happening here!?" It seems that the quantum world has its own

[14] Col 1:15-16 NIV

set of rules and/or physics; quantum physics. And now physicists are trying to 'unpack' the particles and waves they have discovered and determine just what they are and what they are used for in the structure of the universe. This is a daunting task. In fact, these physicists seek particles that some refer to by such esoteric names as "the God particle" (Hicks boson) and other such names, seeking to see how these particles and waves fit into the structure of the universe, and how they contribute to the physical world we all know.

Niels Bohr[15] divided the world into two, the uncertain quantum world and the 'objectifying' world of measuring instruments. Schrodinger's equation,[16] for combining these two worlds (if it were applied) would be one gigantic equation, for it would have to describe not only an electron, but the measuring instrument and the observer looking at the results of the instrument used! Further, it strains our present knowledge to extrapolate the Schrodinger equation to handle the complexity of human consciousness! These quantum measurements contain probabilities that show us the elements of chance revealed in quantum mechanics. So, in this quantum world there is considerably more uncertainty than in the physical world we inhabit. It is this uncertainty that prompted scientists like Heisenberg to formulate his "uncertainty principle."[17] This principle is basically that if we know one thing about a particle, such as an electron, we can't be sure about another thing about this particle. So many measurements that are taken from the quantum world have variable degrees of uncertainty to them. What has been revealed about this quantum fabric of

[15] Danish scientist; contributor to atomic structure and quantum theory (see Bohr model of the atom).

[16] Equation which describes the changes over time of a physical system in which quantum effects are significant. It is a wave equation that is fundamental to understanding quantum physics.

[17] Principle asserting the fundamental limit to the precision with which certain pairs of physical properties of a particle (such as an electron), can be known.

the universe is a significant amount of uncertainty. This is truly horrifying to many scientists, since it suggests to us that there are many things about the very elementary nature of the universe that we cannot know. But this is a comforting 'truth' to me. When I read Psalm 139, particularly verses 6 and 18, where the psalmist proclaims that God's knowledge is "to wonderful for me;" and God's thoughts; "How precious to me are your thoughts, O God! How vast is the sum of them! They outnumber the grains of sand.[18]" God's thoughts are just too far above mine for me to comprehend[19] It seems that the basic fabric of the universe, this quantum world, fits such a description that the psalmist realized thousands of years ago.

Information[20]

Timeless;
Massless;
Space-less;
Energy-less;
It just is.
Invisible,
Immortal,
Information.
"Immortal, invisible, God only wise, in light
inaccessible, hid from our eyes."
(W. Chalmers; 1939)
"In the beginning was the Logos, and the Logos
was with God, and the Logos was God.[21]"

---

[18] Ps 139: 6, 18.

[19] See Isaiah 55:8-9 NIV

[20] D. Poole; 2017. The word 'information is used in this poem as an umbrella term. It is meant to mean many levels of what is considered 'information.'

[21] Logos is Greek for Word. Look it up! John 1:1; NIV

So then, at this basic level, there seems to be a lot of patterns of information that we don't fully understand. Could it be that this quantum world is where all the information necessary to create a physical world exists? Could it be that we are on the brink of discovering the matrix[22] of information that is available for the creative processes that we so glibly go over in the book of Genesis? If so, then we are beginning to 'unpack' a portion of the mind of God (be it rather infinitesimal). Here we sit at the edge of a galaxy and discover the physical laws around us and some scientists go so far as to say that we will have this all figured out some day. HA! What pride. But back to my point. If this quantum mechanics matrix of information is there, what other types of information could be embedded in the fabric of the universe?

I think I need to 'unpack' a little more the ideas above. The ideas that I have hopefully explained a little bit, have a very long history, beginning with the Greek philosopher Plato. Plato was to many people the 'father of philosophy,' and his teachings and precepts have been used as a starting point for many modern philosophies. His basic teaching (from what I can infer) is the Theory of Forms. In that theory he said that there were two basic forms: 1) substance (material things) and 2) ideas – the most accurate form of reality. These two ideas contributed to his allegory of the cave.[23] You may want to look it up. My point here is that ideas are information. Words by themselves represent ideas, and when strung together represent more complex ideas. And we use these ideas to describe and use the material world. Now, let me put that in Biblical context: "The Word became Flesh[24]". Do you 'see' the connection? The idea became the substance. The information became the matter. The Spirit becomes Concrete Matter. Think about it. God has become material in the 'form' of Jesus the Christ.

---

[22] Ground substance, there are 14 definitions for matrix.

[23] From Plato's *Republic* (514a-520a)

[24] Jn 1:14a NIV

Like a lot of old and new testament writers, Paul is attuned to the Spirit and uncovers some of these embedded realms of information in the two verses above, from Colossians 1. Here Paul talks about the creation of things, those in heaven, and those on earth, "visible and invisible." Let's stop right here and look at the meaning in this phrase. We all have a pretty good handle on what the visible part means, but maybe we aren't so sure about the invisible part. Remember, that in Paul's time there were no microscopes or telescopes, or understandings of atoms or cells, or DNA or such. In fact, the science, as you know it, did not exist. I think that when Paul refers to the invisible he has an understanding that there are 'forces' and 'structures' around, which are invisible. He then in the next phrase of these two verses he lists some of the invisible creations as "thrones, OR powers OR rulers OR authorities." It seems to me that Paul's general term for these invisible creations of God is the term 'powers'[25]

Now, 'powers' refers to the 'ordering'[26] of the structures and systems that have been set-up by human societies over time to 'organize' the social world around us. By this I mean governments and authorities that make rules and laws for us to live by and obey (hopefully) to keep us from hurting each other and creating general anarchy. Way back when, Moses set up a system of laws we call the Ten Commandments that the Israelites would use so they could get along together. In more modern times we have set up constitutions for governments and systems of law based on some set of 'rights' or beliefs that are assumed to be 'self-evident'

---

[25] See Romans 13:1; Ephesians 6:12; Hebrews 6:5;1 Peter 3:22 NIV

[26] There is a big difference between 'ordering' and 'ordaining'. God does not ordain the 'powers,' but he has 'ordered' the 'powers.' God has brought order out of chaos from the very beginning of time (See Ge 1:2-3 NIV). God's first 'ordering' was light. Contrast this to 'ordain': to anoint or bless or give authority to something (as the term is used here). God, in creating has 'ordered' most of the universe. That does not mean that these 'orderings' can't be used for evil purposes. God has given the universe freedom to be itself, just as we have freedom to be ourselves.

or mutually agreed upon. But if you notice in history, something goes wrong and each form of government or 'power' (if you will) becomes corrupt or starts to serve other purposes (greed, lust, tyranny) than what it was originally meant to serve, namely the people of that government. So, the question is, what has happened to these 'powers' that they continually go astray?

A good answer lies in the understanding that these 'powers' have "not accepted the **modesty** that would have permitted them to remain conformed to the creative purpose (of God), but rather they claimed for themselves an absolute value."[27] What that means in a nutshell is that those in 'power' (governments) have claimed to have absolute value. In other words, they have become so prideful, that the humility by which they were to rule people has been corrupted by the 'power' they think they possess. These governments have forgotten how to be humble and in doing so they ask for complete allegiance FROM the people rather than having allegiance TO the people. This is my reason why I see so much political 'party loyalty' in spite of morality or religious affiliation. The Church of Jesus the Christ would say these 'powers' have 'fallen.'

So, once we can establish that the 'powers' are lost and 'fallen' in this world, then we can 'see' that something needs to happen to reboot or resuscitate or reinvent these 'powers.' Something needs to stand against them in time and space, as a sign and symbol for change. A sign and symbol are the cross of Jesus the Christ. The church of Jesus the Christ talks about the 'work' of Jesus when he died on the cross. What was this 'work?' First you need to remember that the cross of Jesus cannot be separated from His resurrection. They are one event. Therefore, the cross of Jesus is the unmasking of the 'powers' for what they truly are. The unmasking of the illusion that the 'powers' "have ultimate direction, happiness,

[27] J. H. Yoder; *The Politics of Jesus*, (Eerdmans Publishing Co. 1994) p.142.

and ultimate duty for small dependent humanity."[28] What Jesus brought together in the cross is the mystery that has been hidden (embedded information) in the universe but has come to 'light' in the cross.

Part of this hidden mystery is the unmasking of the 'powers' through the cross. On the cross, Jesus the Christ 'disarmed' the 'powers' and made a public example of them. Jesus the Christ showed for the first time the deception of the 'powers' to seduce humanity. Before the cross, the 'powers' (represented by Pilate and the Pharisees -government and religion) were accepted as the basic and most important realities. Now, in the cross, a new reality has come and its signature is the resurrection. This Christ event announces a New Creation and/or the Kingdom of God, which has broken into our world through the Christ event. Another important idea to notice about the cross of Jesus the Christ is that Jesus died on a cross. This was not some 'magical' act but a concrete physical event. A physical event which changed the universe (see Luke 23:44-45 NIV). A once in a universe singularity, birthing a New Creation. Jesus the Christ has disarmed the 'powers' by striking down the weapon by which they derive their strength: illusion. That is their ability to convince us they were the agents of happiness, ultimate vision, and yes even sacrifice. When in fact, the only true Agent of happiness, vision and sacrifice is God alone. None other.

And this is why you don't hear many sermons on the cross of Jesus the Christ in our churches today. It is too risky. We might anger the 'powers' of today and void our chances of making a more 'Christian' world. We have to submit to the 'powers' of today in order to further our 'Christian' agendas. So, we choose to be 'liberal' Christians or 'conservative' Christians and then we choose to follow our political inclinations of the 'powers' rather than our commitments to our LORD and savior, Jesus the Christ. And we

---

[28] J. H. Yoder; *The Politics of Jesus*, p. 147

do all this in his name! Talk about hypocrisy. And that is my reason why the church is fading into the woodwork today. We don't stand firm! (See Exodus 14:13 NIV)

What does the Church of Jesus Christ need to do today? We need to stand firm and let God do our battles for us. By standing firm our very presence in the world is a threat to the 'powers' of this world. When we allow the 'powers' to rule and influence us, we are not being the Church of Jesus the Christ. We need to demonstrate in our own lives and fellowship how believers can be freed from the 'powers' and not subject to them. We need to reject nationalism and no longer recognize any differences between people because of race, ethnicity or beliefs. Social differences must lose their power to divide. Our duty is **not** to bring the 'powers' to their knees or rebel against the 'powers.' Jesus has already done that. Our duty is to believe that Jesus the Christ is our Lord and hold the 'powers' at a distance (their seduction and eventual enslavement). And we need to learn patience. We need to be still.[29]

If you notice also in the book of Ephesians,[30] where Paul is describing the 'armor of God,' all the armor is defensive. Even the sword of the spirit. (The word for sword used here is "machaira" which is a short sword used for defense.) We are to stand firm with our 'armor' in place and stay close to Jesus the Christ and not within influence of the 'powers.' To be in effect: 'In the world but not of the world.'

As Followers of Jesus today, we are not asked to challenge the 'powers' or collaborate with them. We must remember that the 'powers' are a part of God's good creation, and as such we can only refuse to collaborate with them, siding with the victims the 'powers' are oppressing. The Followers of Jesus are called to be the conscience and servants of human societies. That is part of our standing firm in our faith. I reiterate, we are not called to be

[29] See 1Kings 19:12 NIV

[30] Ep 6:10-18 NIV

'conservative' or 'liberal' Christians, choosing sides in the political arena. We are called to be hopeful, patiently waiting for God to fulfill His promises; His Kingdom. "Thy Kingdom come, Thy will be done[31]."

What is evil?

It was described as the 'biggest massacre in America' when a lone man opened fire from a window in a high-rise hotel in Las Vegas on a crowd of concert goers below. They still don't know the killer's motivation.

May, 2018. There have been many school shootings in America taking many lives, committed by persons who are invariably described by some of their friends and acquaintances as 'normal.' Or comments like: "I never thought in a million years that ____ could do this." More children under 15 years of age are 'killed by bullets' in America, then any other country in the world.

Women getting involved with sex trafficking from 'groomers' who are college professors or in their words "really great guys" that these men methodically trained to be prostitutes for modern day 'pimps.'

What Americans are quite ignorant of is the cloaks that evil uses and techniques of propaganda used to gain our trust. What many Americans don't 'get' is that evil is ordinary. Jesus said: "If you, then, *though you are evil,* know how to give good gifts to your children.[32]" Jesus at the time (Sermon on the Mount) was addressing his disciples. So, when He talks about 'you, then, though you are evil,' is really me and you!

Several quotes from S. Peck's book, *People of the Lie,* are very instructive in understanding 'ordinary' evil. These quotes are used below with short comments from myself.

---

[31] Mt 6:10 KJV (This is the most common way we pray this verse.)

[32] Mt 7:11a NIV

"They live down the street- on any street. They may be rich or poor, educated or uneducated. There is little that is dramatic about them. They are not designated criminals. More often than not they will be 'solid citizens' – Sunday school teachers, policemen, or bankers, and active in the PTSA."[33]

"How can this be? How can they be evil and not designated as criminals? The key lies in the word 'designated.' They are criminals in which they commit crimes against life and liveliness. But except in rare instances- such as the case of Hitler- when they might achieve extraordinary degrees of political power that remove them from ordinary restraints, their 'crimes' are so subtle and covert that they cannot clearly be designated as crimes.[34]" "The predominant characteristic, however of the behavior of those I call evil is scapegoating. They project their own evil on the world.[35]" (They don't see themselves as evil and are good at pointing it out in others.)

"Strangely enough, evil people are often destructive because they are attempting to destroy evil. The problem is that they misplace the locus of the evil. Instead of destroying others they should be destroying the sickness within themselves. As life often threatens their self-image of perfection, they are often busily engaged in hating and destroying that life- usually in the name of righteousness."[36]

"The words "image," "appearance," and "outwardly" are crucial to understanding the morality of the evil. While they seem to lack any motivation to be good, they intensely desire to **appear** good. Their "goodness" is on the level of pretense. It is in effect a lie. That is why they are people of the lie."[37]

"If you are willing to serenely bear the trial of being displeasing

---

[33] M.S. Peck, *People of the Lie,* (Simon & Schuster, 1983) pp.69-75

[34] M.S. Peck, *People of the Lie,* p. 69

[35] M.S. Peck, *People of the Lie,* p.73

[36] M.S. Peck, *People of the Lie,* p.74

[37] M.S. Peck, *People of the Lie,* p.75

to yourself, then you will be for Jesus a pleasant place of shelter." – St. Therese of Lisieux.

What we see here is a 'truth' about evil. Evil wishes to hide itself and appear to be 'good.' It is noteworthy that God also wishes to be hidden from view and 'invisible' in more than just physical ways. What is of value here is to understand that we need to be aware of the spiritual dimension of the universe if we are to truly discern the difference between good (God) and evil. When God created us in His Image, this 'image' was a spiritual creation; since God is Spirit.[38] We were given the ability of discerning 'good' from evil. That was what the story of the garden of Eden was all about, the price we paid to get this 'gift' of discernment. We just need to use it!

Americans live in a society that is not Christian and there are even fewer followers of Jesus. 'Christian' has become a political 'football,' where we have different sorts of 'Christians' lining up on the political left or right, using their political position to make the world a little more 'Christian' depending on their political leanings. In the process of 'moralizing' the world they look for evil in its more virulent form rather than the ordinariness that it is. Evil is cloaked in lies. And many of these lies begin as propaganda and A/NT thinking.

For example, the My Lai atrocity of the Viet Nam War during 1968. You may be thinking: "Why are you going to an event that happened 50 years ago?" Well, during the intervening 50 years since this massacre, there has been a lot written about it, and meaning has been deciphered from this 'experience.' So now, we are in a good place to discuss the meaning of this event in light of what evil is about and its relation to the A/NT pattern of thinking.

The only person convicted of this atrocity was a young second lieutenant named Bill (I will just use his first name, you can look it up), the other soldiers involved were charged but not convicted.

[38] Jn 4:24a NIV

Then, Bill was released from house arrest in 1974.[39] During his trial he said: "I was ordered to go in there and kill the enemy. That was my job that day. That was the mission I was given. I did not sit down and think in terms of men, women, and children. They were **all classified the same**.[40]" Of course, he said more, but my point is in the bold underlined type. There it is: ALL. That sneaky A/NT pattern. If I were to set this up in the form of a thinking problem, here is how I would phrase it: Viet Cong[41] are the enemy. They are Vietnamese. But, not all Vietnamese are Viet Cong. Bill's conclusion: If they are Vietnamese, they are the enemy. Therefore, kill all of them. And that is what he did. And as he said; "I did not sit down and think." I hope I have made my point. Roger Spiller,[42] said; "The most frightening lesson… is that ordinary people can commit heinous crimes under the right circumstances."[43]

And today as we see this scenario of 'ordinary' evil play out over and over again, we scratch our collective heads and wonder 'why?' In my opinion the answer lies with us. Read again the quote above from Roger Spiller. "ordinary people… under the right circumstances." We all carry the 'mark of Cain'[44] within. If you don't believe that **you** can carry out these heinous crimes that we see every week now, then you are blind to yourself. If you are thinking; "I could never do that," notice the use of the A/NT term 'never.' This is another reason why I have come to believe that A/NT thinking can get us into a lot of trouble in our decision making. Also, I believe that when we recognize the darkness within us, we can learn to become a more forgiving community of believers. That

[39] To learn more about this event see- S. Tucker, *The Encyclopedia of the Viet Nam War* (Oxford University Press 2011)

[40] https://www.famous-trials/mylaicourts/1626-myl-calltest This is complete record of testimony. These statements come in the middle of the testimony.

[41] Term used for the North Vietnamese, who were the enemy.

[42] American war historian (1944-2017)

[43] H. Jones, *My Lai,* (Oxford University Press 2017) epilogue, p. V

[44] Ge 4:15b NIV; literally- And the Lord set a mark on Cain.

does not mean that we just forgive anyone who has done these horrible acts of evil in our midst. They need to be held accountable for their acts.

The Constant Gardener

"I am the true vine, and my Father is the gardener. He cuts off every branch ***in me*** that bears no fruit, while every branch that does bear fruit ***he prunes***, so that it will be even more fruitful.[45]" God is our constant Gardener. When and if we 'bear fruit' He prunes us to get more fruit, just as a good fruit tree grower does each year to get more fruit. But what does this 'pruning' involve? Surely God doesn't cut off my arms or legs or any other physical part of me, so this must be a metaphor. What is it then that God prunes IN me, if I am IN Jesus? For me, God 'prunes' my pride and my errors in thinking, forming me more and more like Jesus; helping me have more and more the 'mind of Christ.'

This metaphor also means to me that I must be vigilant. Ready to see the false assumptions that I make about myself and others in my thinking. Ready to catch myself when I fall into one of those destructive thinking patterns that I have described above. Being self-aware is not a one-time thing. It takes practice and patience on a daily basis. To me, it is almost like St. Paul said when he wrote; "Pray continually.[46]" Now, this doesn't mean that we are to get down on our knees and fold our hands and bow our heads (the modern mind), but that we are to be practicing the presence of God in our daily lives on a continual basis, disciplining our thoughts as well as our actions.

The most difficult practice of gardening myself is the practice of 'holding my tongue.'[47] I tie in this idea with what it says in Psalm

---

[45] Jn 15:1-2 NIV

[46] 1 Th 5:17 NIV

[47] Jas 3:2 & 4:11-12. NIV

139: "Before a word is **on my tongue**, you know it **completely**, O Lord.[48]" Notice the emphasis on 'on my tongue' and 'completely.' In other words, God knows what I am about to say (what is forming in my mind) before I say it! This knowledge of God is way above mine, and fearful. God must be inside my head! This means to me, that I need to learn to discipline my thoughts before I can have a good 'handle' on disciplining my speech. Jesus reminds us of this when He says: "But I say to you whoever looks at a woman [or man] to lust for her [or him] has already committed adultery with her [him] in his [her] heart."[49] This statement was Jesus' addition of what the 7th commandment meant.[50] Jesus is telling me that I need to discipline my thought as well as my actions, and that my doing so, I will have control of my actions be it speech or faithfulness to my wife or 'significant other.'

This thought discipline, for me, is a very hard task. I have been 'trying' to practice this for many years now, and I don't seem to have been real successful. Thoughts seem to just 'appear' in my mind, before it seems I have any control of them. I see a pretty woman, who is 'well endowed' and 'BAM', there it is that lustful thought or a critical comment of some sort. How do I pluck out these weeds from the garden of my mind? What seems to work for me (sometimes) is to immediately bring Jesus into my thought world. I say to myself: "What does Jesus see here?" Not 'what would Jesus do.' (Which was a popular phrase for a while). In other words, I am trying to form the 'mind of Christ' in my being, as St. Paul asked us to do. When I have the 'presence' of mind to do that, I find that my thought ascends to a higher level. I see the woman or person that I want to criticize as a person that God loves, just like me, that is deserving of the respect that I myself would like. In other words, the Golden Rule is more likely to be at

[48] Ps 139:4 NIV

[49] Mt 5:28 NIV; my bracketed additions for clarity!

[50] Thou shalt not commit adultery- Ex 20:14 NIV

my mental disposal. This is part of my daily discipline of practicing the Presence of God.[51]

We live in a world where we are constantly bombarded (yes that is the right term) by sex, violence and propaganda of many different forms. We can either go into hiding (recluse, computer games, social media, drugs, etc.) or we can learn to 'be in the world or not of it.'[52] So, as followers of Jesus we need some way(s) to allow this bombardment to go on without participating in its effects on us. We need a 'shield' of some sort. We need some armor of some sort. St. Paul has already suggested it. 'The full armor of God' is a metaphor that St. Paul uses to describe the very thing I am talking about; defenses against this daily bombardment of sex, violence and propaganda.

When I look at the whole metaphor, and not just one part, I imagine myself dressed in armor with a shield, and if I must defend myself, I use words (and hopefully the big one, The Word.) So, for me, the armor is my discernment of truth from lies, and my understanding that I am loved by God, in the most intimate and important ways of life. And I am not willing to let this cultural slavery imprison me. But in order to put this armor and shield on each day, I need some time to prepare myself for the day. Either by meditation, or reading scripture, or praying short prayers. For myself, meditation works the best. But choose your own medicine.

As I have said earlier, we live in a culture of fear. You name it and we have a fear for it. Now, don't get me wrong; we are not going to be able to live this life without fear. The problem is a lot of people don't know what to do with their fear, so they rely on ways of thinking that don't help, in my opinion. They rely on doctors, scientists, technology, comfort food and drink, or social groups or family to alleviate their fears. If you have noticed these ways may

---

[51] For greater understanding see - Brother Lawrence, *The Practice of the Presence of God and The Spiritual Maxims,* (Digireads.com Publishing 2016). Brother Lawrence lived from 1605-91.

[52] Jn 17: 14-15 NIV, summarized.

work for a time, but usually don't solve the problem that fear plays in our lives. There really is only one antidote to fear and that is the 'fear of the Lord.' Wait. I am replacing one fear for another? Well, in a way, yes. And in another way, no. First, we need to understand what 'fear of the Lord[53]' is. You might have heard the phrase: "I fear the Lord, but I am not afraid of Him." And that pretty well says what I mean. I 'fear' God because I know who I AM is. I 'fear' God because I know my place in relation to the King of the Universe. I 'fear' God because I know that my life is in God's 'hands.' That is my 'fear' of God. The 'fear of the Lord' does a very important thing in my life; it creates humility. The 'fear of the Lord' expels narcissism, arrogance, pride, inconsiderateness, indiscretion, and a lot of foolishness (not all, for me, anyway). And this type of fear can replace the other smaller fears in my life, because it gives birth to HOPE. And that hope has been available for a very long time. Millennia's ago, Job said: "Still, I know that God lives – the One who gives me back my life- and eventually He'll stand on earth. And I'll see Him -even though I get skinned alive – see God myself, with my very own eyes. Oh, how I long for that day!"[54]

---

[53] Ps 1:7. NIV

[54] Job 19: 24-27, *The Message.*

ABBREVIATIONS

Books of the Bible

Ge – Genesis
Ex – Exodus
1 Sa – 1 Samuel
Job – Job
Ps – Psalms
Ecc – Ecclesiastes
Isa – Isaiah
Da – Daniel
Mt – Matthew
Lk – Luke
Jn – John
Ro – Romans
1 Co – 1 Corinthians
Col – Colossians
Jas – James
1 Th – 1 Thessalonians
Ph – Philippians

Other Abbreviations

A/NT – All of nothing thinking
ATP – Adenosine Triphosphate (a cellular energy molecule)
AT – Anthropomorphic thinking
DNA – Deoxyribonucleic Acid (the basic molecule of heredity)
ET – Emotional thinking

APPENDIX I
PROPAGANDA

"In propaganda truth pays...It is a complete delusion to think that the brilliant propagandist as being a professional liar. The brilliant propagandist is the person who tells the truth, or that selection of the truth which is requisite for their purpose, and tells it in such a way that their recipient does not think he/she is receiving any propaganda..... The art of propaganda is not telling lies, but rather selecting the truth you require and getting it mixed up with some truths the audience wants to hear.[1]" – Richard Crossman (Deputy Director of Psychological Warfare Division during WWII)[2]

Techniques

Ad hominem: attacking your opponent rather than their argument.

Ad nauseum: repetition of ideas; also, slogans (short emotionally charged statements. i.e.: "blood for oil"; "cut and run;" "lock her up."

[1] http://www.apologeticsindex.org/2910-christian-propaganda

[2] Richard Crossman is an interesting post WWII figure. He served in the British Parliament for several years. Look him up.

Appeal to: a) authority: prominent figure supports your position
b) Fear: instill anxieties or panic in population
c) Prejudice: attach values or moral goodness in your position

Dictate: Tells population exactly what to do (some preachers/ politicians)

Bandwagon: everyone else is doing it....

Inevitable victory: We are going to win, you might as well join us.

Beautiful people: to sell your product or position (therefore, you are beautiful too)

Black & White fallacy: there is only two choices

Oversimplifying: over simplistic phrases
Them or us thinking

Conditioning – Classical: If A is always present then B is present. (i.e.: candidate's picture between Stalin and Hitler)

Operant: Learning through imitation (appealing person using product being sold)

Cognitive dissonance: people desire consistency/symmetry

(For example: if people dislike candidate and like actor A, then show actor A like's candidate.)

Common man: our position is only "common sense" (the average Joe/Jane) of the people.

Cult of personality: Celebrities selling stuff

Demonizing the enemy: those who support the opposing view/ group are less than human. (For example, using any name for an ethnic/political group that puts them down into less than human. Unfortunately, there are already too many.)

Disinformation: falsifying data, forgery

Euphoria: using emotional appeal to boost morale. (Events, holidays, parades)

Flag waving: justifying position by claiming it will make you more patriotic, benefit country.

Foot in the door: quid pro quo: I do a small favor for you and now you are obligated to do one for me. (Unspoken social contract)

Glittering Generalities: emotionally appealing words or stories that apply to the idea, but NO concrete argument for position.

Half-truth: part of a statement is true, but rest is false.

-Quote out of context
-Managing the news: present half-truths repeatedly

Poisoning the Well: Scapegoating/Stereotyping

Labeling: using dysphemism/euphemism (quote a person then label them a 'liberal' or 'right wing'
-Another way of saying "you're guilty by association" (a fallacy)

Latitude of acceptance: modify your position to make more acceptable, then slowly move back to original position.

Love bombing: overwhelm with affection to isolate from another social group (family, etc.).[3]

Obfuscation: intended vagueness, confusion

Straw Man: misrepresenting the opponents position

Testimonial: individual is exploited to further a position/argument

Third party technique: i.e.: hiring a journalist to represent your position; quoting 'independent' sources.

Unstated Assumption: used when an argument or position is less credible. The position is then assumed or implied. i.e.: "Well everyone knows...."

Virtue words: For example: peace, happiness, security, wise leadership, freedom, "the truth". "a religious man" ... etc.

---

[3] This technique is used often by kidnappers and pedophiles.

APPENDIX II

WHAT IS A MIRACLE?[1]

"A miracle is a phenomenon not explained by known laws of nature." (dictionary)

BUT:

1. Frequency of isolated spiral galaxies is about 1/10
2. Fraction of stars in the galaxy located in a region of low local density of stars (between spiral arms and not near its center) is about 1/1000
3. fraction of stars located in galaxy located in a region of high local density of metals is about 1/100
4. Fraction of stars with a mass similar to the sun's mass is about 5/100
5. Formation of a stellar system around the remnants of a second or third generation supernova within a few billion yrs. of the most recent supernova is about 1/10
6. Fraction of planets that are metal rich planets is about 5/10
7. Fraction of planets that have low (relative to asteroid composition) carbon content is about 3/10

---

[1] Most of these probabilities are taken from G. Schroeder, *God According to God,* (HarperOne 2009) pp.76-80.

8. Fraction of planets that have a molten iron rich core is about 2/10
9. Fraction of planets that have low (relative to asteroid composition) water content is about 3/10
10. Fraction of planets with mass (gravity) able to hold an oxygen-rich (but not hydrogen rich) atmosphere is about 2/10
11. Fraction of planets with continent forming plate tectonics is about 1/10
12. Fraction of planets with nearly circular orbits is about 5/10
13. Fraction of planets approximately 150 million km from the sun like star is about 5/10
14. Fraction of planets with huge outer planets is about 1/100
15. Fraction of planetary systems with no huge inner planets is about 1/10
16. Fraction of planets with a period of planetary rotation on the order of days is about 5/10
17. Fraction of planets with a moderate tilt to the planet's axis of rotation is about 2/10
18. Fraction of planets with a large moon is about 5/100

If we multiply all these probabilities than the chance of finding intelligent life supporting planets in our galaxy is 10,000,000,000,000,000,000 to 1. The estimated number of stars in the universe is 10 to the 22 power (10^{22}). This means there may be only 10,000 earthlike planets circling a sun like star. Now there are estimated to be 10 to the 11 power galaxies. That means that we could expect one earthlike planet for every 10 million galaxies!! (do the math). Is life on this planet a miracle?

Other definitions of miracles:

Littlewood (British mathematician): Individuals could statistically expect a miracle (a one in a million event) approximately at the rate of one per month.

Spinoza (philosopher): Miracles are simply law like events whose causes we are ignorant of.

Hume (philosopher): "a transgression of a law of nature by a particular volition of the Deity, or by the interposition of some invisible agent."

James Keller: "If God intervenes to save your life in a car crash, then what was He doing in Auschwitz?" Therefore, God does not perform miracles.

Types of Miracles

Jesus performed cures, exorcisms and natural wonders. God is demonstrating his underlying normal activity in a remarkable way. Cure: Matthew 20:29-34 NIV. Exorcism: Mark 5: 1-20 NIV. Wonder: Mark 11:20-21 NIV.

What about the man born blind in John 9? Only a cure?

Thomas Aquinas: (3 degrees) Highest degree: Something nature does not do. Second degree: something nature can do but not in the same order (man born blind sees). Third degree: Something that is done by nature but without the operation of the natural principle (cure a fever in a short time).

[Some additional scriptures to think about: Exodus 7: 8-12 NIV; Acts 8:9-21 NIV. 2 Thessalonians 2: 9-12 NIV. Revelations 16:12-14 & 19:19-20 NIV.]

ANNOTATED BIBLIOGRAPHY[1]

1. S. Hauerwas & W.H. Willimon, *Resident Aliens* (Abingdon Press. 2014).

    This book was originally published in 1989. And this is the 25th anniversary edition. The book basically tells of the loss of the Christian mission over the last 1700 years. This book is easier to read than Yoder's book on the politics of Jesus. *Resident Aliens* gives many examples and suggestions on how the church can reclaim its primary mission to the world.

2. C. S. Lewis, *Mere Christianity.* (Pte. Limited; 1952; renewed 1980).

    This book is a classic explanation of Christianity by the famous Christian author, C. S. Lewis. It is probably one of his best works. What is outstanding is the clarity of his thinking about the 'principles' of Christianity. It is well worth reading many times, even though some of his references are specifically to England in the early 20th century.

3. Iain McGilchrist,. *The Master and His Emissary* (Hobbs the Printers Limited, 2009).

    McGilchrist is a psychiatrist and researcher in brain imaging and function. This book covers very completely the role that both hemispheres of our brain take on in our daily

[1] These books constitute many of the more recent books that I have read that have helped me formulate my thinking on many of the topics in this book.

thinking. Very complete and well documented. He also relates how history reflects the role of the two brain hemispheres in philosophy and epistemology. This was my source for much of my section of left-brain dominance.

4. Arthur Peacocke, *Paths from Science Towards God.* (Oneworld Publications, 2002).

   Peacocke's book is probably (in my opinion) one of the best books to read on the relationships of God and science. It is difficult to read and must be approached slowly and methodically. This is the last book Peacocke wrote before his death.

5. M. Scott Peck, *People of the Lie* (Simon and Schuster Inc., 1983).

   This book will very likely change your mind if you think there is no such thing as evil. Several case histories are used as examples. Peck also discusses the idea of group evil. I would recommend this book, if you want further information on what is evil and how it shows itself in our modern world.

6. Eugene Peterson, *Eat This Book* (Eerdmans Publishing Co. 2006).

   This a very well written conversation about how to read the Bible. It is part of a five-book series on how to read 'spiritually.' I highly recommend this book, to get a better idea for many of the topics I have covered in this book on seeking higher truth.

7. Gerald Schroeder, *God According to God* (Harper Collins; 2009).

   This book is mainly about how God interacts with us. Schroeder describes his views on the character of God, according to the Old Testament. His main emphasis is on how God partners with us. He integrates science into his views and gives fresh perspectives on the unusual place of humans on planet earth.

8. Gerald Schroeder, *The Hidden Face of God* (Touchstone Books, 2002).

    Schroeder covers many of the controversial topics like brain/mind duality and the basic biology of cells with great insights into biology and it's meaning as it relates to God. He spends a lot of pages explaining metaphysics both from the physics viewpoint and the biological viewpoint. A great read for beginning to understand the hiddenness of God.

9. Gerald Schroeder, *The Science of God* (The Free Press; A division of Simon and Schuster, Inc. 1997).

    In this book Schroeder covers the relationship of science to the book of Genesis, the age of the universe and the logic of the biblical calendar. He presents some unusual solutions to the problems between science and biblical interpretation. This book is well worth the time to read it for gaining new perspectives for the ongoing debate between science and religion.

10. N. T Wright, *The Day the Revolution Began* (Harper Collins Publisher, 2016).

    Wright, as usual, does a very thorough analysis of many of the letters of St. Paul and how they have been misrepresented in history. This book pairs nicely with Yoder's book on the politics of Jesus. His main message is how we have 'Platonized' the life, death and resurrection of Jesus the Christ with a 'wrath of God,' atonement theology, which has distorted our understanding of the mission of Jesus through the centuries.

11. John H. Yoder, *The Politics of Jesus* (Eerdmans Publishing Co. 1994).

    Yoder does an excellent critique of modern Christianity and how we as a religion have been on the wrong track in our theology for the last 1600 years! His interpretation of Jesus' political message is paramount in this book. He is very thorough in his analysis of New Testament scriptures in relation to the politics of Jesus' time.

Printed in the United States
By Bookmasters